**Billy Graham**
Evangelistic Association

1300 Harmon Place, Minneapolis, MN 55403-1988 • 612/338-0500
Internet: www.billygraham.org

Dear Friend:

We are pleased to send you this book, *Generous Living*, as a gift from our
Development Ministries Department at Billy Graham Evangelistic Association.
It is our hope that this book will give you valuable insights that will help make
your personal giving as effective as possible to further God's work.

In this book Ron Blue will help you explore a Christian steward's perspective on
giving as it relates to your situation, the process of giving, and practical applications
for a generous life. We pray that God will provide direction as you involve Him
in opening doors to wisdom and understanding of good stewardship.

If you would like additional information or would like to meet with one of our
representatives at no obligation to you, please contact us at the address or phone
number listed below:

U.S. Residents: Development Ministries
                    Billy Graham Evangelistic Association
                    1300 Harmon Place
                    Minneapolis, MN 55403

                    Toll-free: 1-877-247-2426
                    Fax: 612-335-1244
                    E-mail: devmin@bgea.org

Canadian   Development Ministries
Residents: Billy Graham Evangelistic Association of Canada
                    P.O. Box 841, Stn Main
                    Winnipeg, MB R3C 2R3

                    Toll-free: 1-877-247-2426
                    Fax: 204-943-7407
                    E-mail: devmin@bgea.org

Sincerely,

Franklin Graham

GENEROUS LIVING

FINDING CONTENTMENT THROUGH GIVING

> This Billy Graham Evangelistic Association
> special edition is published with permission
> from Zondervan Publishing House.

Ron Blue

WITH JODIE BERNDT

ZondervanPublishingHouse
Grand Rapids, Michigan

A Division of HarperCollinsPublishers

Generous Living
Copyright © 1997 Ronald W. Blue

⛪ ZondervanPublishingHouse
Grand Rapids, Michigan 49530

Library of Congress Cataloging-in-Publication Data

Blue, Ron, 1942–
    Generous living : finding contentment through giving / Ron Blue.
       p.   cm.
    Includes bibliographical references.
    ISBN: 0-913367-25-7
    1. Christian giving.   2. Generosity—Religious aspects—Christianity.
    I. Title.

Published in association with the literary agency of Alive Communications, Inc., 7680 Goddard Street, Suite 200, Colorado Springs, CO 80920.

Interior design by Sherri L. Hoffman

Printed in the United States of America

It is with gratitude and humility that this book is dedicated to the clients of Ronald Blue & Co.

These men and women demonstrate day to day the joy of living a life stewarding the financial resources that God has entrusted to them. They have written this book by providing an example to me of godly living, and I am privileged to serve them. Thank you, each and every one of you.

contents

Living and Giving with Joy

The amount of money you have has nothing to do with financial security or contentment. Neither can satisfaction be found in wise investments, careful budgets, or debt-free living. Instead, the secret to financial freedom and joy is directly linked to one thing: the willingness to be generous with what you have.

Generosity

The Secret to True Contentment

W HEN THIS BOOK WAS STILL IN ITS INFANCY, I flew to Grand Rapids, Michigan, for a meeting with my editor at Zondervan. As I settled into my seat on the airplane, I couldn't help but notice the young woman next to me. She was attractive, well dressed, and looked about twenty years old. But what struck me more than anything was the discontented, almost angry look she wore. Rarely had I seen a stranger look so unhappy.

"Where are you going?" I asked, trying to start a conversation.

"Grand Rapids," she replied, before focusing her gaze on the magazine she carried. Clearly, she did not want to talk.

I glanced at the magazine. It was one of those in-flight travelers' catalogues, offering everything from designer luggage to fancy electronics. As I turned my attention to some paperwork, the young woman continued to scrutinize the catalogue. Finally, after about thirty minutes, she reached for the cellular telephone in the seat in front of us. She ran a credit card through the phone and began punching numbers.

My curiosity aroused, I looked to see what she was up to. Credit card in hand, my young seatmate was systematically working her way through the catalogue, ordering something, it seemed, from almost every page. Never had I witnessed such a thorough (and expensive) shopping spree—to say nothing of the cellular phone bill!

Thirty minutes later she replaced the telephone. I realized this young woman obviously had money to burn. I stole another glance at her face.

She looked just as unhappy as ever.

The picture of that young lady stands in sharp contrast to the images I have in my mind from another trip. Just before I began working on this book, my wife Judy and I flew to Japan, where we visited our daughter, Karen, and her husband, Mark. We traveled through various parts of Asia, touring through Hong Kong with some missionary friends. We happened upon Hong Kong as the city was gearing up for the Chinese New Year festivities. The celebration, we were told, was like an American Thanksgiving, Christmas, New Year's, and Fourth of July all rolled into one. Business came to a halt as hundreds of millions of revelers traveled throughout China and Taiwan to join their families and friends.

In Hong Kong itself, the streets were mobbed. We found ourselves swept along with the crowd, weaving our way through thousands of vendors hawking everything from chickens (both live and dead) to finely tailored suits and all manner of electronics. Everywhere we went we were surrounded by high-rise apartments. Stretching skyward from the crush of humanity and dinginess below, the buildings heightened my sense of claustrophobia. As I looked up at the endless lines of laundry flapping from balconies and strung between buildings, I wondered how many people made their home in each one of the apartments towering above us?

I thought about Karen and Mark's apartment in Japan, which was small—about five hundred square feet. The shower stall was in the kitchen—but, as Karen laughingly pointed out, that didn't matter much since the bedroom was only another half step away. The only real discomfort was the cold. Without a central heating system, it might be as cold as twenty degrees Fahrenheit indoors in the morning, before the space heaters were turned on.

A friend had arranged for the four of us—Karen, Mark, Judy, and me—to stay at the Ritz Carlton in Hong Kong. It was a real treat. In Karen's eyes, though, the hotel stay seemed less than remarkable. Like each of my children (and most of their generation), Karen tends to see folks my age as much better off, financially, than she and her peers will ever be. To Karen, it made perfect sense that Judy and I would find ourselves camped in a fancy hotel.

Sometimes I wish I could take my kids back in time, so they could see where we've been. The father they see now is the man who has spent the last seventeen years building a large financial and investment counseling firm. They see the author, the radio commentator, and the public speaker who gets dubbed a financial "guru." When I speak, they hear me get introduced sometimes as "the guy who is going to give us all the answers."

But that's only part of the picture. What my kids cannot see is the reality of my own childhood, my growing up in post-Depression Indiana. Neither of my parents went to college; my mother only finished the eighth grade. Dad worked in a factory to provide for our family. Instead of renting a beach house or a mountain cabin, we took vacations in relatives' homes. Instead of going to theme parks or ball games, we packed picnics for weekend entertainment. And instead of buying new clothes or toys, my brother and I made do with hand-me-downs. I'll never forget the broken baseball bats we taped and tacked back together!

I attended a public high school and then worked my way through Indiana University, waiting tables in my fraternity and borrowing money to pay for my room and board. By the time I finished graduate school in 1967, I had a wife, one child, several thousand dollars worth of school debt, and an ancient turquoise Chevrolet.

I landed a job with a national CPA firm, and Judy and I moved east to New York City. With almost no furniture and even less cash, we used credit to purchase a hide-a-bed and a chair for our modest apartment. Two years later I got transferred, and we loaded up the bed and the chair, along with all of our meager possessions, and moved to Dallas. We found a home we wanted to buy. The only problem was that we had no money—not even for the down payment. We got a loan for ninety percent of the home's price and asked my father to borrow the other ten percent for us.

Three years and as many moves later, I left the national firm and started my own CPA practice in Indianapolis. I was twenty-eight years old. Thanks to the booming real estate market, Judy and I had made money on each of our houses, but it was not enough to launch a business. To get the company started, I had to go into debt.

Soon, though, the business began to grow—and with it, our income. I was thirty, Judy was twenty-eight, and we had two young children. We moved to a larger home and joined a country club. To all appearances, we looked like a "successful" young family—yet I was far from being financially "free." Most of the money I made was funneled right back into the business. Then, too, we felt the pressure of all the debt we still carried from our furniture, our home, the business, and the two car payments we made each month.

We joined a socially "acceptable" church, which we attended more often in the winter than during the summer months, when I preferred to spend Sundays on the golf course. For me, church was primarily a place where I could network and develop business contacts. Judy and I also regarded our church affiliation as being "good for the kids."

But things began to change later that year. Judy developed some medical problems that, the doctors told us, brought her within hours of dying. Understandably shaken by the experience, she began to wonder what would have happened had she died. She decided to ask our minister—who, she soon realized, had no idea how to answer her questions.

About that time a neighbor of ours invited Judy to attend a Bible study. She went—and discovered a place where people had answers and talked openly and confidently about their faith. Judy wanted what these women had. When the opportunity to accept Christ as her Lord presented itself, Judy grabbed hold of it. She became a Christian.

As Judy grew spiritually, she became dissatisfied with our church and asked if I would attend another one with her. It made no difference to me. What did bother me, though, was her asking what I thought about the Bible and about Jesus Christ.

To me, the question posed a serious threat to the safe, socially conscious world I had created. I turned on Judy and very nearly exploded. "I know more about the Bible than you do," I charged. "I went to a Christian elementary school, and I've been in church all of my life. The Bible is not relevant for today—and if you continue down this road you've chosen, well, I just don't know what it might mean for our marriage!"

I now know that my anger back then was born out of conviction. But Judy did not argue with me. Instead, she held her tongue, saying almost nothing about her faith for two years. She continued to study her Bible—and, reluctant as I was to admit it, I could not help but notice the change in her life.

For starters, she had a vitality and a joy that seemed almost constant, even when things did not go her way. My love affair with golfing—once a source of bitter conflict between us—suddenly seemed not to bother her. Instead, when I played the game three or four days a week and came home long after our young children were asleep in bed, she seemed genuinely accepting of my priorities. I saw golfing with clients as a necessary part of building a successful business, and Judy was determined not to challenge me.

Perhaps the most telling change, though, was when Judy signed up for a Lay Institute for Evangelism. Part of her training involved going door-to-door in the community, talking to complete strangers about her faith in Jesus Christ. *Wow,* I thought as I watched her go, *that's not the same woman I married.*

While all of this change was taking place in Judy's life, I continued to attend our new church with her on a semi-regular basis—although I only went to Sunday school and never sat through one of the minister's sermons. Week after week the Sunday school teacher opened the class by telling us that if we were not Christians, we would not understand his message that day. He quoted Scripture to support this assertion. I scoffed at the idea. After all, I reasoned, I was intelligent and obviously successful. Hadn't I achieved every financial goal I had ever set in my life? I figured it didn't take much to follow the weekly ramblings of a kindly Sunday school teacher.

And in one sense, I was right. Each week the teacher managed to work something called "The Four Spiritual Laws" into his lesson, and I could quote them from memory: *God loves you and offers a wonderful plan for your life; Man is sinful and separated from God; Jesus is the answer to the separation problem;* and *We must individually receive Jesus Christ as Savior and Lord and enter into a relationship with him.* I knew these laws like I knew my own phone number—but I had little idea what they really meant.

One day, though, I noticed an evangelism tract that included the four spiritual laws lying on my bedroom dresser. (To this day, Judy maintains that she did *not* put it there!) I was on my way out the door to play golf, and I pocketed the tract. Later, alone in the car en route to the golf course, I read through the four laws again. I knew they were true. Unwilling to jump in with both feet, I nonetheless made a conditional commitment to the Lord: "I believe in Jesus and I accept him as my Savior," I said. "But I'm not going to change my life!"

I was not trying to be flippant or stubborn. Instead, I reasoned that if what the Bible said about Jesus was really true and I accepted it, then my life would change on its own, without my forcing the issue or putting on some kind of "religious" act.

I was right—but I wasn't prepared for how quickly the change would take place. After playing the first few holes of golf that afternoon, I suddenly realized I had stopped swearing. I had never been particularly guarded in my vocabulary at any time, but on the golf course, in particular, I tended to overdo it. Now, though, I was amazed at the change.

Likewise, my desire for alcohol disappeared. My whole way of looking at life, in fact, took a dramatic turn. Where I had once been consumed with the pursuit of worldly wealth, social recognition, and power within the business community, I began to value my time with my family more and more—to the point where I almost resented my business contacts and commitments on the golf course. And although I never "announced" my spiritual transformation to Judy, she spotted the difference, marveling at how the stress level—in my job and within our family—had plummeted.

Meanwhile, the business I had started continued to thrive. Day after day I sat behind an impressive mahogany desk in an expensive office, calling the shots on all manner of financial decisions. To say that it was not stimulating would be untrue—but when Judy and I got involved in a city-wide evangelistic campaign, I realized that my daytime activities could not compare to the work we pursued each evening during the crusade. I was in charge of the telephone center located in a warehouse. We had set up phone banks in the vast empty room to take calls from people who saw the campaign on television. Each night, sitting behind my stark metal desk in the barren warehouse, I tallied the results as our evangelism team ministered on the telephones to callers from all over the city. Humble as it appeared, I knew that my ugly metal desk saw far more significant "profits" than its daytime mahogany counterpart.

As Christians, we wondered what sort of lifestyle we should lead. *How should we provide for our family? How much should we give to the church or other ministries? Where should our children go to school? What should we think (and do) about debt? How—and how much—should we pay for clothes, vacations, camps, sports, and college? And what about retirement?*

Judy and I began to pray about a career change. After several months, we sensed God calling us to leave the Midwest and move to Atlanta to work full-time in ministry. We knew the change would be dramatic. When we arrived in Georgia, we had four children, a smaller, twenty-year-old house, and only twenty percent of the income we had grown accustomed to in Indiana.

And we had a whole new set of questions to answer. As Christians, we wondered what sort of lifestyle we should lead. *How should we provide for our family? How much should we give to the church or other ministries? Where should our children go to school? What should we think (and do) about debt? How—and how much—should we pay for clothes, vacations, camps, sports, and college? And what about retirement?* As we struggled to address issues like these from a spiritual—rather than secular—perspective, we felt as though we were starting all over again.

After two years in the ministry, I again felt the Lord's leading to make a career move. Unwilling to subject our children to the callous materialism that had marked our lives in Indiana, Judy and I decided to stay in Atlanta, where I used my accounting background to launch a firm that would provide financial and investment counsel from a biblical perspective. The idea was to equip Christians to be wise stewards of the resources God had given them. Even as I worked with our clients, however, the questions remained. I could show other people how to budget and invest effectively, yet I still felt a personal sense of insecurity.

Guilt cropped up as I wrestled with supporting the poor and needy—while I sent my own children off to expensive summer camps and signed them up for tennis and piano lessons.

As the questions spun around and around in my mind, they gave rise to an uncomfortable sense of fear, guilt, and frustration. Fear manifested itself with questions like *What happens if . . . ?* and *Will I ever be able to afford . . . ?* Guilt cropped up as I wrestled with supporting the poor and needy—while I sent my own children off to expensive summer camps and signed them up for tennis and piano lessons. And the frustration mounted as, month after month, I struggled to get "control" of my money, wondering whether or not it was already too late to pursue and achieve my financial goals—goals like providing for my children's education and building a nest egg for retirement.

Almost everyone I met grappled with these same kinds of questions, regardless of how much money they had. Most people also struggled with the negative emotions—fear, guilt, and frustration—to some degree. But that didn't make the feelings any more right or desirable. There *had* to be a better way. Instead of fear, I wanted freedom. Instead of guilt, I wanted joy. And instead of a confused frustration, I wanted order, confidence, and peace.

How could I make the move?

FINDING FREEDOM, JOY, AND CONFIDENCE

THE ANSWER CAME OVER TIME AS I talked with, counseled, and observed, our clients. Over the years I have had the opportunity to work with a number of very wealthy individuals. Many of these people are genuinely happy. Yet the key to their freedom, joy, and confidence is not their money. Having the cash to buy or do whatever you please does not guarantee contentment—the young airplane shopper was living proof of that.

Likewise, the secret to financial freedom is not couched in wise investments, meticulous budgets, or debt-free living. All these things are valuable—yet even the highest investment return or the most carefully constructed budget affords very

little in the way of real confidence and joy if one key ingredient is neglected. That one ingredient—and the ingredient that
makes true freedom possible—is generosity: the willingness
to use your time, talents, and material wealth to benefit others and impact eternity.

**Having the cash to buy or do whatever you please
does not guarantee contentment.**

I have spent more than a quarter-century studying financial and investment strategies. I've written several books and
spoken to countless people via television, radio, and in person.
I am, as I mentioned earlier, often introduced as "the guy with
all the answers." But if I could boil down everything I have
ever learned into one sentence or thought, it would be this:
Generosity and financial freedom are inextricably linked.

The Bible supports this principle. "Give, and it will be
given to you," promises Luke 6:38. "He who gives to the poor
will lack nothing," says Proverbs 28:27. And, according to
2 Corinthians 9:6–7, "Whoever sows generously will also reap
generously . . . for God loves a cheerful giver."

Many of our firm's clients are living, vibrant examples of
this truth. The folks who enjoy genuine freedom and joy are
those who give the most, relative to their incomes. Giving is
more than just a way to use your money. It is a lifestyle, a way
of living that allows you to hold all that you own—including
your time and your talents—with an open, generous hand.

This book is designed to get you to that place. I want to
challenge you, philosophically, to evaluate your willingness and
ability to give. I want to teach you how to make sense out of
all the requests for your money, your time, and your talents so

you can maximize the effectiveness of your giving. And I want to show you how to instill a generous spirit in your children and build a legacy that will last.

If I could boil down everything I have ever learned into one sentence or thought, it would be this: *Generosity and financial freedom are inextricably linked.*

Practically speaking, I want to help you decide how much to give—to your children, to your church, and to charity. I want to give you the tools you need to make your plan work, through family conferences, wills, trusts, and other techniques.

I want to move you from fear to freedom, from guilt to joy, and from frustration to confidence. I want to help you ungrasp your hand.

There will always be legitimate needs: poor people to care for, churches to support, and missions to build. But instead of feeling guilty or frustrated by our inability to meet all these needs, we can feel confident, joyful, and secure. It all depends on where our treasure is. It all depends, that is, on what we truly want to attain.

Treasure Hunting
Where is Your Heart?

I SLOWLY SPUN THE GLOBE NEXT TO MY DESK, MY FINGERS tracing a path across the Atlantic Ocean in the general direction of Africa. "Mauritania," I muttered under my breath. "Where *is* Mauritania?"

I looked across the room to my two visitors. One man represented a well-known international relief organization. His companion served as the organization's country director for Mauritania. Together, they had come to my office to ask for my financial support of their ministry.

In a moment my search was rewarded. I found Mauritania on the coast of West Africa, a tiny country encompassed almost exclusively by the Sahara Desert. It was, my guests told me, a nation marked by extreme poverty. Ninety-nine percent of the people were Muslim.

Right away I felt guilty. I realized I would spend more on a business suit than a person in Mauritania would need to live on for an entire year—and I had nine suits hanging in my closet! I knew the physical and spiritual needs my visitors described were legitimate, yet I couldn't escape a sense of frustration, and even anger, over the fact that these two strangers would come to ask me for money. I didn't even know where Mauritania was!

And it wasn't just them. Not a week goes by when our mailbox isn't stuffed with fundraising appeals, prayer letters, and other requests for help. Almost all of them, I suspect, represent genuine needs from people whose faith and value system parallel my own. Yet I don't even open all the letters. I know I will feel guilty or angry if I do.

I am not the only Christian who struggles with the whole issue of giving. I know I'm not. Whenever I take calls on a radio program, review the questions submitted by magazine readers, or talk with folks personally when I speak in public, the number one and two topics are always debt and tithing.

Should I tithe if I am in debt? Should my tithe go to the church, or someplace else? How much should I give? When I look at my paycheck, should I tithe off the gross or the net? What about the money I made when I sold my house or my stocks—do I tithe off of that? What if my wife/husband does not want to give?

The questions go on and on. People simply do not know how they should give, where they should give, or even why they should give.

The requests we get for money—in untold numbers every year—can generate guilt, frustration, and ultimately, anger.

And it's no wonder they are ignorant. Almost nobody teaches about giving these days. Today's preachers—the most likely candidates for the job—are often gun-shy when it comes to the subject of giving. I can't say that I altogether blame them. I think I might be reluctant, too—at least when I consider the reactions I'd be likely to get.

There are always unlimited ways to use limited resources.

My attitude about the relief workers who came to my office is fairly typical, I would guess, of how many people feel toward giving. The requests we get for money—in untold numbers every year—can generate guilt, frustration, and ultimately, anger. Here's what I mean: Say you get a letter or a phone call alerting you to a need—whether it's halfway around the world in a place like Mauritania or just across town in the local homeless shelter. You know you could always lower the bar on your lifestyle, living on less to give more money away. Maybe you start to wonder about your priorities. Is it okay to send your daughter to summer camp or buy yourself a new car? Would that money be better used for the needy? You are not sure—so you choose to ignore the questions. Or you feel guilty.

The one thing we do know is that there are always legitimate needs. There will always be poor or sick people to care for. There will always be churches, Christian schools, and missions to build and support. There will always be those who do not yet know Christ. It would be nice if we had unlimited wealth to use in solving these problems. But there are always unlimited ways to use limited resources. As a result, we encounter frustration.

Together, guilt and frustration can give rise to anger. *Why, we may wonder, did they call or write to me? (I do not even know where Mauritania is!) Why doesn't their church or mission group*

pay them enough? Why doesn't that homeless guy get a job? Why
does everyone always need money? Why is the job never done?!

In chapter one I told you that the most joyful, contented,
secure people I know are the givers. How, then, can I expect
you to reconcile that observation with all the guilt, frustration,
and anger I've confessed to in the last few paragraphs? How
can I expect you to give?

It all comes down to where your treasure is. It all comes
down to having a heart like Ruby's.

THE WOMAN WHO COULDN'T OUT-GIVE GOD

RUBY STARED AT HER DAUGHTER in disbelief. "How bad is
it?" she asked.

Ruby's daughter had quit her job teaching kindergarten to
learn more about the business her father, Bob, had started
some fifteen years earlier. The company manufactured water
treatment chemicals, and although neither Ruby nor her
daughter knew anything about chemistry or running a business, they figured it was time to start learning. Bob had been
diagnosed with cancer and was not expected to live.

Ruby knew that business had been slow, but nothing could
have prepared her for her daughter's report. The company,
which had been generating very little income, had unpaid bills
that were thirty-six months overdue! Unwilling to burden his
wife with the bleakness of their situation, Bob had kept the
indebtedness a secret.

Ruby felt numb from the shock. First, she had had to
accept the very real probability that her husband—who was
already too sick to get out of bed—would die. Now, she realized, there was a good chance she would lose the business as
well. She could think of nothing to do except pray. As she

knelt before God, she half expected him to tell her what a wonderful woman she was, and that he shouldn't be doing all this to her. Instead, she heard simply one word.

Give.

Ruby knew what the Bible said about giving. She knew that it said things such as "Give and it shall be given to you" and that it offered promises about how God would pour out his blessings on people who gave. As the Lord spoke, Ruby understood that he intended for her to take these promises seriously. He wanted her to give.

Right away Ruby went to her husband's bedside to ask for his permission. Could she, she wondered, ask his secretary to write a business check to their church?

"Go for it," Bob said, figuring they had nothing to lose.

The next morning Ruby went to her husband's office and instructed the secretary to write a check for one thousand dollars. *It might as well have been a million*, Ruby thought. She had no idea where the money would come from.

The secretary protested. "We're not going to do that!" she exclaimed. "That doesn't make any sense at all—there's no money in the account. And even if we had the cash, we've got a whole stack of big bills to pay!"

Ruby knew she faced strong opposition. The woman had held her post for seven years and knew the business better than Ruby did. She probably considered Ruby a well-meaning, but ignorant, meddler.

"If you want to keep your job," Ruby said evenly, "you'll write that check."

"All right," the secretary conceded. "It's no skin off my nose if you want to lose the company."

A week later Bob died. Ruby forgot all about the check. It was not until a month later that she even revisited the business she had inherited. When she did, she dedicated the failing company to the Lord. "Whatever you give to us," Ruby vowed, "we will give back to you in tithes and offerings—ten percent plus."

When she finished praying, Ruby paid a visit to the secretary. "Whatever happened to that check we wrote to the church?" she asked.

"Ruby," the secretary replied, "you won't believe this. There was enough money in the account to cover it—although I don't know where we got the funds."

"Write another one."

The secretary stared at her new boss. "Never!" she exclaimed. "Bob would not have done that."

Again, Ruby prevailed. And again, there was money available to cover the check. In fact, for the next year Ruby contributed one thousand dollars per month, ever mindful of God's command to "give." And every check cleared—even when Ruby thought there was next-to-nothing in the bank.

The business began to flourish. Within a year all the overdue bills had been paid and the company was in the black. Ruby decided it was time to increase their giving to two thousand dollars per month. This time the secretary did not protest.

Year after year Ruby raised her monthly giving, slowly at first and then with bigger jumps. Today the company gives away twenty thousand dollars each month. Not long ago a banker reviewed the company's accounts. Noting Ruby's pattern of generous giving—even when there was not enough cash to meet all the company's bills—he simply shook his head. "I don't understand it," he admitted, "but you must be doing something right."

The stories Ruby tells of how God has met people's needs through her giving are nothing short of remarkable. One time, for example, she could not shake from her mind the image of a young, single mother she recognized from her church. The woman's name was Sheila; beyond that, Ruby knew very little about her life or her financial circumstances.

As Ruby prayed for Sheila, she sensed that the woman had a financial need. "How much?" Ruby asked the Lord.

God gave Ruby a specific dollar amount. She wrote the number down and then contacted the church's assistant pastor. "Does Sheila need any money?" she asked.

"Not that I know of," the pastor replied. "Why do you ask?"

Ruby recounted her story, telling the pastor the amount she thought Sheila needed.

As it happened, the pastor and his wife had already planned to have dinner with Sheila that very evening. Sheila seemed perfectly fine—until part way through the meal, when she broke down in tears. "I need so much," she confessed. "I haven't wanted to burden anyone with my problems, but I don't know where to turn."

As Sheila divulged her concerns, the pastor grabbed a notepad and said, "Tell me exactly what you need and how much you think everything will cost."

Somewhat puzzled by the request, Sheila nonetheless began listing her needs. "The roof leaks," she said, "and the lawn mower is broken."

"What else?"

Sheila ticked off several more pressing financial problems, tagging each one with a rough estimate of what it would cost for replacement or repair. When she finished, the pastor totaled the numbers and stared, almost speechless, at his pad. He couldn't wait to call Ruby.

He saw her at the post office the next morning, even before he had a chance to make the call. "Ruby!" the pastor cried. "You're not going to believe this. Remember how much money you thought Sheila needed? You were right—right down to the penny!" Laughing with delight, the pastor swung Ruby around right there in the post office, oblivious to the scene they created.

Since then, Ruby and Sheila have become close friends. "It's amazing what God can do with a life when you give everything to him," Ruby observes. "If he has your heart, he automatically has everything—including your money. You just don't hold anything back."

GIVING WHEN IT DOESN'T MAKE SENSE

LIKE RUBY'S SECRETARY OR THE BANKER who questioned her financial priorities, many of us might look at a situation such as the one Ruby faced after her husband died and put giving last on the spending list, if anywhere. Certainly we would want to purchase food, clothing, and other things our family needed first. And from a strictly economic standpoint, we'd be correct. Logically speaking, giving never makes sense.

For one thing, we can never meet all the needs. Like a drop in the ocean, our dollar or two (or even thousand dollars or two) will hardly be noticed in the grand scheme of things. Viewed in this light, our giving may seem pointless.

Moreover, we may question where the money will come from. Rarely do we feel financially able to give generously toward a newly recognized need while continuing to fund the people or projects we already support. Like robbing Peter to pay Paul, we would have to shortchange somebody—no matter how valid the need.

Finally, no matter how much money you have or what tax bracket you fall into, you can never gain financial ground by giving. Even when you factor in the deductions for charitable contributions, you'd still be better off, financially, if you simply kept all the money for yourself. It always costs money to give.

Giving costs—but therein lies the point. When Jesus talked about giving, he applauded those who gave what they could not logically afford to give. He reserved his praise for those who gave extravagantly—regardless of the amount of the gift. Ruby is not the only widow whose story stands as a powerful example of extravagant—and seemingly senseless—giving. Consider the poor widow whose offering the Lord commended in Mark 12:41–44.

I can imagine the scene. Jesus sat across from the temple treasury, watching people make their contributions. Many rich people, dressed in fine clothes, approached the offering box with a sense of religious pomp and ceremony. The Bible says they "threw" their money in—noting, I would guess, the satisfying "ch-ching" the coins made as they fell.

Then a poor widow came along. She probably went almost unnoticed in the hustle and bustle that marked the temple courtyard—and she probably liked it that way. Unlike her wealthy neighbors, she could not afford to make a hefty donation. In fact, she could not really afford to give anything. But still she came, hoping (I imagine) to slip unobtrusively alongside the money box and quietly drop in her offering—two small coins that were all but worthless.

Unwilling to embarrass the woman, Jesus did not make a scene. Yet he called his disciples to his side to let them know what the woman had done. "The truth is that this poor widow gave more to the collection than all the others put together. All the others gave what they'll never miss; she gave extravagantly what she couldn't afford—she gave her all" (Mark 12 *The Message*).

For that woman, two cents was everything. The Lord singled her out—both from the temple crowd and from all the other examples in Scripture. The poor widow's story stands as the only direct reference Jesus makes to the manner in which Christians should give. That widow, like Ruby, gave God all that she had.

WHAT GOD WANTS FROM YOU

DO STORIES LIKE RUBY'S and the biblical widow's mean we need to empty our savings accounts into the church coffers? If we want to be commended by God, must we literally give *all* that we have?

Regardless of your particular passion, your treasure is what you think about, what you go after, what you want to attain. It's where your heart is.

No and yes. No, we don't need to fork over our life savings. God does not need our money. True, he commands—and expects—us to give, but our money is not what he's really after. What God really wants is our heart.

To me, one of the most significant verses in the Bible is Matthew 6:21: "For where your treasure is, there your heart will be also." Your treasure is the thing that is most important to you. Maybe it's a job promotion, a new house, or a new car. Maybe you want to get married or have a child. Maybe you just need a vacation, and you dream about soft white beaches and vibrant sunsets. Regardless of your particular passion, your treasure is what you think about, what you go after, what you want to attain. It's where your heart is.

Looking back, I can honestly say that there was a time when my treasure was couched in the recognition and success I achieved in business. When I became a Christian, though, those priorities began to change. My heart turned toward my family, and I began to think more about their eternal destiny than about our material needs and desires. My heart—and my treasure—was no longer bound up in money and worldly ambition.

What about you? God knows your heart can't be devoted both to him and to wealth or material pursuits. You cannot, as Matthew 6:24 puts is, serve both God and money. God does not say it's *difficult* to serve both. He does not say we should try *really hard* to serve both. He says it's *impossible* to serve both. You must make a choice.

God asks you to give because he wants your heart. Your behavior says a lot about what you truly believe. How do you feel about giving? Do you really believe God loves a cheerful giver and that he will reward your generosity? Can you hold your treasure—your money, your possessions, your time, your talents—with an open hand? Are you willing to give him your heart?

If your answers to questions like these point to a need for a change, you need to know that the transformation will come as a process. Generosity doesn't happen overnight. But God does promise us this: if we seek him first, and keep on seeking him first, everything else—food, clothing, and all of our needs—will be taken care of (see Matthew 6:33).

Yes, then, we do have to give God our all. When we give God our heart, he has our treasure—and everything else that we claim. That way, when people from Mauritania—or any-place else—walk into your office, you don't need to feel guilty, frustrated, or angry. Instead, you can be free. Your treasure belongs to God. How you use it is, ultimately, up to him.

All God asks is that we be good stewards of the resources he gives us. Good stewardship means making wise decisions regarding how you use your money—from how much you spend on your children to how you maximize the effectiveness of your contributions to church and God's work. If you have given God your heart—and if how you behave truly reflects what you believe—then read on.

Good stewardship means making wise decisions regarding how you use your money.

The idea is not to get you to simply empty your pockets. Nor is it to hand you some kind of magic number or formula to get you to figure your "tithe." Instead, the coming chapters will teach you how to give generously and wisely. God asks us to give. Our job is to step out in obedience and faith.

As a nation, Americans could give away an extra $100 billion per year without even feeling a pinch—but statistics show we are getting stingier than ever. Why don't we give more? Sometimes it's simply a matter of a lack of vision, ignorance, or poor planning.

three

Why Christians Don't Give

Seven Things that Hold Us Back

OVER THE PAST YEAR OR SO, A NUMBER OF NEWS-paper and magazine articles have found their way into my stack of reading material, each one telling its own version of the same eye-catching story under headlines such as these: *"Generation awaiting its $10 trillion inheritance," "The new way to get rich,"* and *"Why the inheritance boom is for real."*

The stories stem, at least in part, from a report issued by two Cornell University economists. Their landmark study, published in 1993, got baby boomers drooling over what would soon be theirs: the largest collective inheritance in world history.1 This unprecedented wealth transfer—estimated at anywhere from $8 to $14 trillion—has had business and investment gurus, government policymakers, and the boomers themselves all worked into a lather over the opportunities and challenges such a dramatic windfall represents.

So what will the boomers do with the jackpot? Economic analysts predict that much of the money will be used for debt retirement, with some being spent on what they call "vanity purchases": a new BMW, exotic trips, cosmetic surgery, and other "self-oriented stuff."2 In general, the experts say, we are about to witness a major shift from the savings-oriented lifestyle of the post-World War II generation to one that is marked by spending and consumption.

There's no question that, as a nation, we are a consumptive group. In 1994, for example, we spent $500 million on wrinkle cream and twice that much, a billion dollars, on sunglasses. We coughed up $634 million for golf balls. We spent $12 billion on weight-loss programs—which isn't all that surprising, when you consider that we ate a whopping $79 billion worth of fast food![3]

"So what?" you may say. So what if we spend $79 billion a year on burgers, shakes, and fries? After all, America is by far the largest producer of goods and services the world has ever known. We are a wealthy country; we've got the cash. So what if we spend it?

On an individual basis, the more we make, the less we may tend to give.

The problem isn't really how *much* we spend on sunglasses, golf balls, or cheeseburgers. The trouble is how *little* we spend, relatively speaking, on the things that matter so much more. In the same year that we sat around eating all those french fries and smearing our faces with wrinkle cream, we spent just $2 billion on foreign missionary work.

Let me put that in perspective. Assuming that about 90 million of us actually go to church (out of the 150 million who claim church affiliation), giving $2 billion per year to missions works out to about $23 per person. Less, in other words, than we'd spend on one pair of good sunglasses, a dozen golf balls, or a couple of trips through the drive-thru.[4]

Why? Why do we care so much about our own needs, here and now, and so little about others and their eternal destiny? Are we really all that self-centered and stingy?

I heard a radio talk-show not long ago in which a caller claimed people would give more if we had more. If we got a break in our taxes, she said, we'd have more money, and we'd give a lot more to our churches and charitable organizations like the Salvation Army.

"Oh, there's no question about it," the radio host agreed. "No question at all."

The talk-show host and his caller echoed a refrain I've heard over and over again. "I'd like to give more," people say, "but with a mortgage payment and groceries to buy and three kids to put through college and credit cards to pay off—well, there just isn't any extra! If we had any extra, I'd give it—but right now, we just can't."

America's private sector could donate at least $100 billion more *per year* than we already do—and with a minimum of sacrifice or risk.

Folks who rely on logic like this may mean well, but, unfortunately, the statistics tell a different story. Sitting on my desk is a thick report entitled *The State of Church Giving through 1994*. From 1968 through 1994, the study shows, U.S. per capita disposable income increased by 54 percent, after taxes and inflation were factored out. During that same time period, our giving as a percentage of our income declined by 21 percent. In other words, while our incomes rocketed skyward, our giving, percentage-wise, took a significant hit.[5]

| 1994 Giving Results | | |
Income	Average Gift	% of Income Given
Under $10,000	$ 207	2.7
$10–19,999	332	2.3
$20–29,999	668	2.7
$30–39,999	715	2.0
$40–49,999	572	1.3
$50–59,999	632	1.1
$60–74,999	1,572	2.3
$75–99,999	1,720	2.0
$100,000 and above	3,213	3.2

Source: Gallup Organization, Inc.
(Source Note: Data appeared in *Giving and Volunteering in the United States*,
which is published by Independent Sector.)

FIGURE 3.1

And, on an individual basis, the more we make, the less we may tend to give. As figure 3.1 shows, a person who makes $15,000 per year is apt to give away more than twice as much, percentage-wise, as someone who makes $50,000. (Neither gives away anything close to the ten percent tithe discussed in the Old Testament, but 2.3 percent looks a whole lot better than 1.1 percent!)Is it really that we can't afford to give? Are we really so buried under our own mortgage payments, grocery bills, and education needs that we can't give anything away? Not if you believe Claude Rosenberg Jr.

Rosenberg spent years researching and analyzing America's giving abilities and habits. His findings, published in his book *Wealthy and Wise*, indicate that most of us give away less than ten percent of what we could actually afford to—without jeopardizing our financial security or making significant lifestyle sacrifices.

Rosenberg's findings confirm what I've secretly suspected for years. In working with our clients to develop financial plans and giving strategies, I have intuitively felt that they could probably give away far more than either of us might have guessed. Yet I was not prepared for how *much* more we could give. According to Rosenberg, America's private sector could donate at least $100 billion more *per year* than we already do—and with a minimum of sacrifice or risk.[6] So why, then, if we truly can afford to give an extra *billion* dollars, why are we not *more* generous?

WHY WE DON'T GIVE MORE

THE "WHY" QUESTION IS ONE I have wrestled with for years. I am often asked to speak to ministry groups and their donors, and as I prepare for these talks, the "why" question always factors into my thinking. I figure if ministries understand why Christians don't give, they will be better equipped to help potential givers overcome the obstacles. And, for the donors themselves, I like to think that my analysis will motivate them to give more by addressing the specific issues that hinder their own generosity.

There are seven reasons why Christians don't give. Illustrated, they form a pyramid that looks like this:

Why Christians Don't Give

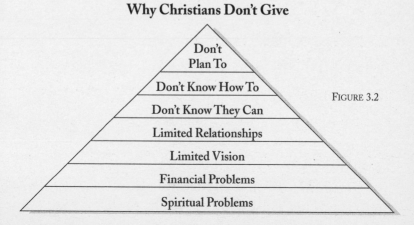

FIGURE 3.2

On the first (and most basic) level, Christians don't give because of *spiritual problems*. They don't have the right belief system, from a spiritual perspective, toward money. Church and parachurch leaders—and really, anyone who is involved in teaching and discipleship—need to communicate what the Bible says about money, ownership, and the eternal rewards promised for those who live and give generously. We always act on what we believe. Therefore, our beliefs must be anchored in the truth.

As we are developing our belief system, the first thing that crops up to squelch our generous spirit is the reality of present *financial problems*. We don't know how to handle money wisely—as evidenced by things like the $4,010 in credit card debt the average American household owes today.[7] Add that to car payments, mortgages, college loans, and the like, and it's not hard to see why we feel financially strapped. Money is tight— and until we learn to spend less than we earn, it always will be.

The first thing that crops up to squelch our generous spirit is the reality of present *financial problems*.

Third, Christians fail to give because of a *limited vision*. I remember a call I got from a parachurch organization that wanted me to donate $100,000 to their work. I was flattered they thought I had that much to give. The truth was, however, I had only a fraction of that amount—and, more importantly, I only had what I call a "$100 vision" for their ministry. I did not know a lot about the organization, and I was not convinced that a hefty contribution on my part would constitute wise stewardship. In the end, I decided not to send them anything. It was too embarrassing to send a check for $100 (my vision) when what they'd asked me for was $100,000 (their vision). But I learned an important lesson that day: We will never out-give our vision.

Just as Christians need to develop a vision for giving, we also need to expand our *limited relationships*. If pastors, development officers, and others in Christian leadership would recognize that people give where they have relationships, their financial appeals would be far more effective. I once heard a pastor say that people remember more about how you make them feel than about what you actually say. If that's true (and I believe it is), then if folks in your church or ministry are not giving, it may be because they don't feel like they are really part of what's going on.

> **If pastors, development officers, and others in Christian leadership would recognize that people give where they have relationships, their financial appeals would be far more effective.**

The fifth reason why people fail to give or live generously is simply that they *do not know they can.* As Rosenberg asserts, most of us can afford to give far, far more than we already do. Most of us could double, triple, or even quadruple the amount we give now—we just don't know it. We don't know how much we owe, much less how much we actually own. We have only a general feel for what's in our savings accounts, retirement plans, or life insurance policies. Likewise, we rarely sit down to consider our long-term goals and figure out how we plan to reach them. It's no surprise then that we so quickly dismiss the thought of giving with the simple excuse that we cannot afford it.

Of course, some of us will eventually take stock of our
finances long enough to realize that yes, we could make room
in the budget for giving. At that point, the obstacle to generosity may simply be that *we do not really know how to give.*
When the Goodwill truck rumbles its way through our neighborhood, we gladly clean out our closets—but we don't always
get a receipt (or we lose it before tax time rolls around). When
the stock market goes up, we hang onto our profits, oblivious
to the tax-wise techniques we could use to give the appreciated
assets away—without sacrificing any liquidity or jeopardizing
our cash-flow position. And, when we finally get around to
making our will, we fail to provide for charity along with our
heirs—and we could wind up losing in excess of 70 percent
of our assets to taxes and other fees! In short, we don't understand the giving tools and strategies covered later in this book.
As a result, we give ineffectively, or not at all.

**Unless we plan ahead, we will only be able to give the
leftovers, if anything.**

Finally, *we don't plan to give.* We plan for retirement or for
starting a business or for funding our children's education, but
few of us have a plan for giving. There will always be unlimited
ways to use our limited resources, and—unless we plan ahead—
we will only be able to give the leftovers, if anything. Even an
increase in our salaries won't make any difference. Needs always
expand to meet income. (By contrast, we've found that as our
firm helps people plan for the future, giving typically increases
fivefold, in terms of the actual dollars our clients give away!)

So where do you stand? Is your giving hampered by your
belief system or by the burden of unwanted financial prob-

lems? Do you find yourself wondering how much you could *really* afford to give? Are you frustrated when the needs you see or hear about exceed your vision—or your pocketbook?

In the coming chapters you'll meet people who have successfully dealt with issues like these as they've scaled the pyramid of problems. I'll introduce you to a man who found a way to give away fifty percent of his income—and still provide for his family's needs, put five kids through school, and retire by age fifty-five. I'll tell you about a couple who were on the verge of complete financial ruin and bankruptcy before they got a handle on their problems and became two of the most faithful givers I know. And I'll show you how to structure your estate so as to minimize taxes and maximize the amount you can leave to your heirs and to charity.

Today, some seventy percent of Americans die without a will. As a result, the government collects thousands, hundreds of thousands, and even millions of dollars in estate taxes—when, in most cases, simple estate planning could reduce that amount to *zero*. If your estate—your home, your life insurance, your retirement plan, etc.—is valued at less than $600,000 (or $1.2 million for a couple), you should pay nothing in estate taxes. *Nothing.* That's the 1997 tax-fee limit. According to new tax laws, this limit will increase every year up to $1 million by the year 2006. In other words, married couples, as of 2006, will be able with proper planning to transfer at least $2 million without owing any federal gift or estate taxes. And regardless of the value of your estate, by including charitable giving and other tax-wise techniques in your estate plan you can reduce taxes, increase your giving, and, in some cases, *increase* the amount you leave your heirs.

You may look at the pyramid in figure 3.3 and realize you don't have a vision for giving, or you're stuck in a web of financial problems, or you don't know how to give effectively. But that doesn't mean you can't, ultimately, enjoy the rewards of generous living. Generosity is not something you wake up one day and simply "decide" to do or be.

Instead, as the pyramid suggests, generosity is a mountain of sorts. As with any climb, you need to start at the bottom. The foundational issue—your spiritual perspective—is what will make your steps secure. A pyramid can never be any stronger than its base. As you begin the trek toward generosity, start by evaluating the strength of your personal belief system.

As you climb higher and higher, don't be surprised if you notice fewer and fewer hikers on the hill. Not everyone makes it to the top of the mountain. Generosity involves more than money. It requires time, energy, and a commitment to staying the course—assets that not every climber is willing to give.

But if you start to feel weak-kneed, remember this: When you reach the peak of the pyramid, the view from the top is magnificent! When you've conquered your financial problems, built your vision and relationships, and used the right tools and techniques to make your giving effective, you will have maximized your potential for generous living. Standing on the summit, you'll feel you're on top of the world!

Of course, as all serious climbers know, there's always another mountain. For those who would live generously, this realization comes as an invigorating challenge. Once you've climbed that first pyramid, you'll find yourself craving the view from other, higher peaks. On these successive adventures, your journey won't be so much of a pyramid as a *process*.

The Process of Generous Living

If you can look at the pyramid in figure 3.2 and pinpoint the obstacles to your individual giving, you can also study the giving process and chart your own course through the mountain range. There's no clear-cut "finish line"; instead, the process is more of a cycle you can use over and over again, regardless of your income level or how much, percentage-wise, you give away. Here's how the process works:

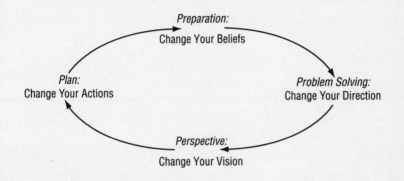

FIGURE 3.4

The first stage in the cycle is *preparation*. You prepare your heart and your mind for giving by *hearing God's Word*. Before you can make any sound financial decision—whether you want to buy a home, invest for retirement, or support a missionary in Mauritania—you need to know what the Bible says about money and how to handle it. You need to anchor your belief system in the Truth.

Next, you have to solve your *problems*. Difficult financial situations—such as an overwhelming amount of debt or an inability to get ahead—are often symptoms of underlying problems. These deeper issues may involve wrong thinking, bad attitudes, or poor decision making. I wrote a book entitled *Master Your Money* specifically to help people think rightly about money, make wise decisions, and get control of their finances. I'll talk more about handling financial problems in chapter 6, but if you want more information, please see the resource list at the end of this book.

Third, you have to put things in *perspective*. God is always at work around you, but how and when you recognize his handiwork depends on where your heart is. If you want to maximize your giving and make it effective, you must work to establish the relationships and contacts that will give you a *vision* for God's work.

Difficult financial situations—such as an overwhelming amount of debt or an inability to get ahead—are often symptoms of underlying problems.

Finally, you must have a *plan*. Giving is more than just a one-dimensional decision; it involves forethought, commitment, and *action*. People who think they cannot afford even a ten-percent tithe typically discover they could give much more than that if they planned to. I like to look at giving on three levels: what you *should* give, what you *could* give, and what you *would* give. To attach a specific price tag or percentage to these three levels, you have to answer some tough questions about your lifestyle and your priorities—questions like *How much is enough?*

Helping you answer these questions and develop your own strategy for generous living is what this book is all about. Understanding the giving process—the *preparation,* the *problem solving,* the *perspective,* and the *plan*—is critical to your success. In part 2 of this book I'll teach you the principles behind each step in the process, with real-life illustrations to show you how to put them into practice.

First, though, I want to introduce you to a component of the generosity process that has nothing to do with your finances. Generosity should not be confined to your checkbook; instead, you can reap the benefits of a generous lifestyle every day, everywhere—in your workplace, your community, and your home.

Take a moment to look back over the pyramid on page 43. Think about why you give—and why you don't. If financial problems or a limited vision is holding you back, you can move closer to generosity by broadening your understanding of the term. Generosity, as you'll discover in the coming chapter, is not about money. It's an *attitude*—and when you have it, it impacts every area of your life.

Today, it's often easier (and always more con-venient) to write a check than it is to share our time or our skills. But opportunities for generous living surround us every day—we just have to know how to take advantage of them.

four

Generosity as a Lifestyle

*Giving Time, Talents,
and Possessions*

IN WINSTON-SALEM, NORTH CAROLINA, AN OLD
stone church fits snugly between the city's newcomers: bank
buildings, hotels, and an eclectic mix of shops and restaurants.
Parking spaces are in short supply, and on Sunday mornings,
churchgoers must arrive early if they want to get a good spot.
Each week, the pastor gets there before anyone else. But
instead of pulling into the best parking place, he drives past
the church to a parking lot located several blocks away. By
walking a few blocks back to the church, he leaves the closer
space open for someone else.

In Lawrence, Kansas, a single mother and her nine-year-
old son move into an old house, eager to spruce it up and get
themselves settled. On the first sunny Saturday they decide to
tackle the front yard, pruning overgrown shrubbery, mulching
flower beds, and raking leaves that have been on the ground
for months. They have only been working a short while when
their next-door neighbors appear with a leaf blower and offer
to help. Together, the group makes good progress, but as the
afternoon wanes the mother finally has to quit. She had

promised to take her son out to dinner; the lawn will have to wait. The neighbors understand—but instead of packing up their leaf blower, they opt to stay and finish the job.

In Bermuda's Horseshoe Bay, a newlywed couple peers down through turquoise-clear water as a school of brightly colored fish darts between their ankles. They have had a delightful honeymoon—thanks, in large part, to the hospitality of a seventy-year-old Bermuda resident. The man, who has a long history of volunteer work with a U.S.-based Christian ministry, freely and frequently offers the guest apartment in his home to other ministry workers—most of whom could never otherwise afford a Bermuda vacation.

In each of these true stories, the common thread is generosity: the willingness to give or share what you have to benefit others. The walking pastor, the leaf-blowing neighbors, and the hospitable Bermudan all sacrificed valuable resources—time, convenience, talents, and possessions—in order to serve other people. Today, when it is often easier (and always more convenient) to write a check than it is to share your time or your skills, gifts such as these become all the more significant.

In the last chapter, we looked at seven reasons why Christians don't give, ranging from spiritual and financial problems to the lack of a concrete plan for financial generosity. When it comes to sharing things like time, talents, or possessions, we can likewise point to a variety of factors that limit our generosity: busy schedules, family duties, professional commitments, and even a general wariness about becoming too involved in other people's lives—particularly when the other people are strangers.

All of these factors, though, stem from one basic problem. The main reason we fail to exercise generosity in our daily lives is because we have a sinful, self-oriented nature.

The Bible points to the universality of our fallen condition. In Romans 3:23, for example, Paul reminds us that "all have sinned and fall short of the glory of God." Likewise, Isaiah 53:6 says, "We all, like sheep, have gone astray, each of us has turned to his own way" (see, for example, Rom. 8:28 and Isa. 53:10). We want to do things for ourselves—and modern society does little to redirect our focus. Media headlines rarely applaud selfless acts of service; instead, we admire men and women who have attained power, prestige, position, and material wealth.

At home, we raise children with an eye toward making them "the best": the best students, the best athletes, and the best achievers. At work, we strive to reach the top: to move up the ladder, make more money, and gain recognition from our peers. In our communities, we want to be out in front of the crowd—and we have little time or respect for people we pass along the way. There is a bumper sticker that seems to sum up our collective mentality: "If you're not the lead dog," the sticker warns, "the view never changes."

What would Jesus say to this widespread preoccupation with self-promotion? Probably the same thing he said to his followers two thousand years ago: "If anyone would come after me, he must deny himself," and "If anyone wants to be first, he must be the very last, and the servant of all" (Mark 8:34; 9:35). If we want to follow Christ, in other words, we must live a life marked by self-denial and service to others.

At the outset of this book I told you that financial freedom comes with holding material wealth with an open hand. For many folks, that may seem like a contradiction: we would feel a lot more secure, we tell ourselves, if we knew our money was squirreled away in a high-performing mutual fund. It's the same way with generous living. We *think* we would be happy if we had a more manageable schedule or a better job or a vacation where we could "get away from it all." In our minds, self-gratification is tied up with personal fulfillment, contentment, and joy. In reality, though, true fulfillment comes when we practice a generous lifestyle—manifested by a willingness to share our time, talents, and possessions.

We know when we are being financially generous—it is evidenced by the dents in our checkbooks. Opportunities for generous living, on the other hand, may be more difficult to track or record. But they are no less plentiful. In fact, the prospect of generosity meets us every day; all we need to do is to recognize and take advantage of it.

SHARING TIME, TALENTS, AND POSSESSIONS AT HOME

WHEN OUR CHILDREN REACHED THEIR EIGHTH birthdays, I took them on a special getaway, just the two of us. Judy did the same thing with each child when he or she turned thirteen. The trips were not lavish or long; instead, the main point was to spend time together, away from the routine and distractions of everyday life.

Looking back, Judy and I have fond memories of these getaways. At the time, they were sometimes difficult to pull off: we had to rearrange our calendars, save money for the trips, and spend long hours planning the itinerary with each of the children. But the relational rewards that came with being generous with our children far outweighed any cost involved.

We will always have things to accomplish; our schedules are packed with everything from marketing meetings and corporate lunches to laundry piles and unpaid bills. Our "busyness" makes the opportunities for generous living almost impossible to recognize. But if we look at our schedules in light of Christ's emphasis on self-denial and service to others, our priorities will fall into their proper order.

Susan Yates, a popular author and family-conference speaker, tells the story of how she learned to reorder her priorities and be more generous with her time. One evening, as Susan confronted a stack of unpaid bills, one of her daughters asked for a back rub before bed. Susan decided to tackle the bills first, as the job had been on her "to do" list all day. But by the time she sealed the last envelope and made her way upstairs to her daughter's room, the girl was fast asleep. Susan realized, with a sinking feeling, that her commitment to her "to do" list robbed her of the opportunity to share and talk with her daughter during one of the day's few quiet moments.

A few days later, Susan's son announced he had a school report to do on Abraham Lincoln. He wanted her to drive him to the nearby Lincoln Memorial so he could get some "inspiration." Susan was busy with her own writing. It was on the tip of her tongue to deny her son's request when she changed her mind. This time, instead of putting her own schedule and desires at the top of the priority list, she put her son first. The two of them spent a couple of hours walking around the Lincoln Memorial, talking the whole time. The experience might not have helped the school report, but today it stands out in Susan's mind as an instance of time well spent.

In addition to giving time, you can be generous in the way you speak to your family members. Think about what you say to your spouse and the tone of voice you use when you talk. Are you quick to nag, belittle, or criticize? Ephesians 4:29 says, "Do not let any unwholesome talk come out of your mouths, but only what is helpful for building others up according to their needs, that it may benefit those who listen." Instead of tearing down your spouse or your children with sharp words, take advantage of opportunities for praise and affirmation. In addition to building your spouse's or children's self-esteem, your liberal use of kind and encouraging words will significantly improve the climate of your home.

Your home can also be used as a launching pad for sharing talents and possessions. Do you cook? Fix a meal for one of your neighbors. Are you handy with home repairs? Lend your talents to someone less skilled. Do you have a spare bed? Offer to house an exchange student or a visiting missionary through your church.

Sometimes the little things are the most powerful tools for turning a self-oriented focus into one that seeks to identify and meet the needs of others.

The possibilities are endless. Start by taking an inventory of the things you own and the skills you have, and then look for opportunities to share these assets. Offer to baby-sit for a young mother, or invite some neighborhood children to your home for story hour. Share your lawnmower, your hedge clippers, or your gardening expertise. Practice generosity toward other family members: let someone else take a shower while the water is still hot, or use the sink before you do. Offer to do another person's chores. Give away the last piece of chocolate cake.

Ideas such as these are so simple that they almost sound silly—but don't underestimate the importance of how your actions will impact your children. Later in this book I'll tell you about the advantages of passing on more than material wealth to your heirs. A generous spirit is part of the legacy you can give your children, so as you practice generosity, teach them to do the same: Encourage older siblings to help younger ones with homework or household chores. Praise them when they take the time to help a younger or less skilled child learn to roller-skate, dribble a basketball, or read. Work together as a family to create a special surprise for someone who needs an extra measure of love. When a child says, "I'm bored," encourage him or her to find creative ways to use his time and talents to bless someone else. Sometimes the little things are the most powerful tools for turning a self-oriented focus into one that seeks to identify and meet the needs of others.

GENEROUS LIVING IN THE WORKPLACE

LIKE THE HOME, THE WORKPLACE IS ripe with opportunities for generous living. Acts of service can be as easy as holding the door open for someone or allowing another person to use the copy machine before you do. Self-denial may mean skipping your lunch break to help a coworker with a project or working a few extra hours to get a job done ahead of schedule to, by your promptness, make someone else's job easier.

Proverbs 25:11 says, "A word aptly spoken is like apples of gold in settings of silver." Look for ways to affirm your colleagues. Take the time to let someone know you appreciate his or her work, or write a simple note to thank a coworker for his leadership, dependability, innovation, expertise, or willingness to see a difficult project through to completion. A note doesn't have to be long or especially well written—what counts is your sincere expression of respect.

Even if your job situation is less than ideal, you can still practice generosity. Don't expect your boss to be perfect. Instead, give him or her the benefit of the doubt, and take care to honor your superiors through your behavior and your conversations.

If you are a manager, take time to listen to your subordinates. Remember to commend them to your superiors, giving them full credit for their accomplishments. When you hand out assignments, be generous in allowing plenty of time to get the job done. Even if something is not due for a month, your employees will be grateful for the consideration you show towards their schedules.

If God owns everything, then your time, your skills, and your business ultimately belong to him.

Proverbs 3:27 says, "Do not withhold good from those who deserve it, when it is in your power to act." If you own a company, see to it that your employees have good benefits. Be generous with raises and bonuses, and consider adding a flex-time option to the workday so employees can structure their schedules to better accommodate the demands of work and family. Be alert to your employees' workloads, and give an occasional extra day off to someone who needs it.

If God owns everything, then your time, your skills, and your business ultimately belong to him. How you handle these resources reflects your true priorities, commitments, and beliefs.

GIVING YOURSELF TO YOUR COMMUNITY

SHARING YOUR TIME, TALENTS, AND POSSESSIONS at home and in the workplace is often easier than giving these assets to people you do not know. But sometimes the opportunity for sacrificial giving—sharing with others at a cost to yourself—is greatest in your community, among your casual acquaintances and even perfect strangers.

Remember the story of the good Samaritan? As Jesus tells it in Luke 10:30–37, a Jewish man was headed from Jerusalem to Jericho, and was attacked by robbers, who beat him and left him for dead. The priest and the Levite who saw the man first hurried by, pretending not to notice his plight. They were important religious figures with demanding schedules; their time serving at the temple was too valuable to "sacrifice" on one half-dead Jew.

But then a Samaritan—one of a group of people who did not even associate with Jews—came upon the man. Not only did he stop, but the Samaritan went out of his way to bandage the man's wounds, put him on his own donkey, take him to an inn, and pay for the care he would need to receive. The Samaritan rearranged his entire schedule for a complete stranger, giving his time, his medical skills, his donkey, and his money.

At the very center of generous living is an awareness of the preciousness, or value, of other people.

How often do we pass roadside accidents or disabled vehicles, too busy to stop and offer our assistance? How often do we pull out in front of someone in traffic, or race to snag the better parking place? How often are we too full of our own self-importance to return the grocery cart, hold the elevator, or politely say good-bye to a dinnertime telemarketer instead of just hanging up the telephone?

At the very center of generous living is an awareness of the preciousness, or value, of other people. When you begin to see people as God sees them, giving your time, talents, and possessions—even to folks you do not know—becomes a natural expression of your relationship with Christ.

You don't have to look far to find opportunities for sharing your resources in your community. Schools thrive on the efforts of parent volunteers; urban children flourish under the influence of adult mentors; food banks, homeless shelters, and other missions could not operate without the sacrificial giving of our time, skills, and possessions. Start by putting the chips you decide not to buy back on the proper shelf in the grocery store, then work your way up to sacrificial generosity by looking for ways to make a difference in your community.

GETTING STARTED: A FIVE-STEP PLAN

JUST AS HAVING A FINANCIAL PLAN can help you free up more money for giving, so having a lifestyle strategy can help make generosity a reality in your life. Five action steps can help you identify, and take advantage of, the opportunities God gives you:

1. Examine your priorities. Start by reexamining your priorities, reminding yourself of the value God places on other people. Philippians 2:3 says, "Do nothing out of selfish ambition or vain conceit, but in humility consider others better than yourselves." Think about the things that matter to God, and put those items (or people) at the top of your list.

2. Inventory your assets. Make a list of what you have to offer: your time, your talents, and your possessions. According to Romans 12:6, all of us have different gifts or talents. Whether we are skilled at serving, teaching, planning, leading, or something else, our job is to share our gifts with others. And just as financial resources must be managed carefully, so these assets must be used effectively to serve others. Don't waste your resources; instead, be prepared to use them when the opportunity arises.

3. Ask the right questions. When someone asks us to give our time, skills, or possessions to a particular group or cause, we often respond with the wrong questions. Instead of asking, "Is it convenient for me?" or "What do I get out of it?" start by asking whether or not God would want you to use your resources—*his* resources—in this way.

4. Eliminate expectations. When you give time, talents, or possessions, be sure you do not expect to receive anything in return. Don't do your good works as the Pharisees did, in order to "walk around in flowing robes and be greeted in the marketplaces, and have the most important seats in the synagogues and the places of honor at banquets" (Mark 12:38–39). Instead, remember that sacrificial giving involves a cost to yourself, not a reward for your generosity.

5. Give your schedule to God. Start each day by giving your schedule—your calendar, your appointments, your plans—to God. Ask him to show you how he wants you to use your time, and give him the freedom to interrupt your agenda.

Start each day by giving your schedule—your calendar, your appointments, your plans—to God.

Lifestyle generosity doesn't happen overnight. Instead, it's more of a growth process: the more you give, the better you feel—and the more joyful and contented you are, the more you want to give. In the coming chapters, we'll cover the various phases in the generosity process. As you work your way through the cycle, you'll discover how generosity—in your finances and in your lifestyle—really is the key to freedom, satisfaction, and contentment.

PART two

The Process of Giving

The Bible says that money is a tool, a test, and a testimony. How you handle your own resources depends on understanding these concepts and then taking the time to discover, firsthand, what God wants you to do with the money he gives you.

five

Preparation
Hearing God's Word

SALLY FOUND HER HUSBAND SITTING ON THE BACK porch of their new home, sobbing. "What is it?" she asked, fear choking her voice.

"I don't know," Jim replied. "It's like I have this big ache inside, and I don't know how to fix it."

Sally stared up at the stars. She and Jim had a good marriage and three beautiful young children. Jim had met all his career goals, having earned a strong reputation as well as a healthy salary. They had just finished building a large and gracious home. What more could anyone want out of life?

"I just don't know," Jim repeated. "All I can do is pray that God will help me."

Jim had grown up in a Christian home, but he knew very little about giving. In fact, Jim realized, he had become much more concerned about making money than giving it away. As he contemplated the size and value of his new house, he couldn't help but wonder whether it was somehow wrong to enjoy such material comforts. Could it be that the home itself was the source of his discomfort? If so, he was prepared to call the movers!

Jim decided to ask me what I thought. A colleague of his had referred him to our firm, and Jim and I had become good friends. He seemed eager to learn and apply what the Bible says about financial management—including the parts about giving. Unfortunately, when he asked me whether or not he should live in such a nice home, I could not give him an easy answer.

"What do you think God thinks?" I asked. "Are you spending time asking God the questions you're asking me?"

When Jim admitted that it was difficult for him to find time for God, I challenged him to spend just ten minutes each day reading the Bible. Even if it meant getting up a little earlier than he was used to, I knew the extra moments would pay off, particularly since Jim truly wanted to know God's will for his life. Financially, he recognized that God wants Christians to be good stewards of their resources—but Jim was not altogether sure what that really meant, at least not in a very practical sense.

I told Jim that wise stewardship begins with an understanding of ownership. Who, I asked, really owns your house, your possessions, your money? When Jim seemed unsure how to respond to my question, I finally spelled out the answer for him. "It's God," I said. "God owns it all."

"Show me where in the Bible it says that!" Jim challenged.

To prepare yourself for generous living, you need to find out what God says about money.

For starters, we looked at Job 41:11, where God tells Job, "Everything under heaven belongs to me." Then I turned to Haggai 2:8: "'The silver is mine and the gold is mine,' declares the LORD Almighty." Finally, we read 1 Chronicles 29:14. As he watched the Israelites bring forth hundreds of tons of precious metals and gemstones for use in building the temple, King David prayed, "Who am I, and who are my people, that we should be able to give as generously as this? Everything comes from you, and we have given you only what comes from your hand."

King David understood what Jim was still trying to comprehend. *Everything* that we have—our houses, our cars, our money, our jobs, our families, our very lives—comes from God.

This principle is an integral part of the generosity process. It is part of the very first step in giving: *preparation.* To prepare yourself for generous living, you need to find out what God says about money. It's just like I told Jim: *You need to hear the Word.*

WHAT THE BIBLE SAYS ABOUT MONEY

I REMEMBER TRAVELING WITH an American missionary, who was working in Kenya several years ago. As we drove along in his jeep, he confided to me that he was having difficulty providing for his family. The money always ran out before the end of the month, leaving him unable to even purchase food and other basic necessities for his wife and three daughters. Increasing his salary was out of the question, as the organization he worked for put strict limits on the amount that missionaries could receive from their financial supporters.

I began by asking the man where he spent the money he earned.

"Right off the top," he said, "I give thirty-six percent of it away."

I was intrigued. "Tell me more about that," I said.

"Well," the fellow explained, "when I was younger I went to a youth conference where the speaker challenged us to start tithing, and then increase our giving by one percent each year. I began by giving away ten percent, like the man suggested, and ever since then I've upped my giving every year. I've been doing this for twenty-six years."

I had to mask my astonishment. Here was a fellow giving away substantially more money, percentage-wise, than most Christians I knew—yet his motivation for giving was way off the mark. God commands us to give, to be sure, but he also says we must take care of our families. "If anyone does not provide for his relatives, and especially for his immediate family," says 1 Timothy 5:8, "he has denied the faith and is worse than an unbeliever."

For my missionary friend, giving had become no more than a ritualistic response to a teenage commitment. I encouraged him to think about whether or not he was using the money God gave him in the right way. Had form, I wondered, replaced faith? Was he violating a scriptural principle—providing for his family—in order to comply with a self-imposed rule?

As I reflect on what the Bible says about money, I believe Scripture points to three ways money can be used: Money is a tool, a test, and a testimony.

Money Is a Tool

We are not to hoard money, serve it, or pursue it as anything other than a means to an end. Instead, we are supposed to *use* it. Moreover, since all that we have comes from, and ultimately belongs to, God, every decision we make—from giving to missions to buying new sneakers—has spiritual implications. As we consider our spending, the question we need to ask ourselves is *Am I using my money—my tool—the way God wants me to?*

Money Is a Test

Money may also serve as a *test*—financially, practically, and spiritually. The writer of Proverbs grasped the significance of this truth when he wrote, "Give me neither poverty nor riches, but give me only my daily bread. Otherwise, I may have too much and disown you and say, 'Who is the Lord?' Or I may become poor and steal, and so dishonor the name of my God" (Prov. 30:8–9).

Since all that we have comes from, and ultimately belongs to, God, every decision we make has spiritual implications.

Thomas Carlyle, the British historian and essayist, said, "Adversity is hard on a man, but for one man who can stand prosperity, there are a hundred that will stand adversity." Prosperity is a test that most people cannot pass.

The church at Laodicea is a case in point. Founded in 250 B.C., Laodicea became famous for its fertile fields, beauty, and wealth. The city served as a center for banking and finance, even minting its own coins. By the latter part of the first century, when the book of Revelation was written, the Laodicean church had apparently grown accustomed to this affluence, putting material wealth ahead of spiritual needs.

Prosperity is a test that most people cannot pass.

And for this they reaped the Lord's rebuke: "I know you inside and out, and find little to my liking. You're not cold, you're not hot—far better to be either cold or hot! You're stale. You're stagnant. You make me want to vomit. You brag, 'I'm rich, I've got it made, I need nothing from anyone,' oblivious that in fact you're a pitiful blind beggar, threadbare and homeless" (Rev. 3:15–17 *The Message*). The Laodiceans allowed wealth to replace faith, and thus failed the test of prosperity.

Today, our faith faces a practical test each year when it comes time to fill out our tax returns. Working with clients over the years, I think I've seen and heard it all. Almost everyone resents paying taxes. Yet Jesus commanded his followers to pay what they owed to Ceasar—and believe it or not, the Roman Empire was *much* worse, in terms of greed and corruption, than our government is today!

When you look at your tax return, it's easy to gauge your spiritual perspective. For example, how much you spend on interest compared to how much you give says a lot about what you believe. You get a tax deduction for the interest as well as the charitable contributions—but only the interest deduction points to a lifestyle funded by debt. Look at your deductions. Do you take a greater deduction for interest on debt than you do for your charitable giving?

Money Is a Testimony

In addition to being a tool and a test, money is a *testimony*. Not everyone, of course, has access to your tax return. But most people can see, at least to some degree, how you spend your money. How you use it is a direct reflection of what you believe. If you truly believe that everything comes from God, you will use your money to accomplish his purposes—and that will stand as a testimony to the world.

The early Christians we read about in the book of Acts spent their time proclaiming the good news of Christ's resurrection, sharing their wealth and possessions so that not one of them was needy or poor. "From time to time," Acts 4:34–35 says, "those who owned lands or houses sold them, brought the money from the sales and put it at the apostles' feet, and it was distributed to anyone as he had need."

Like their fellow believers, Ananias and Sapphira had the opportunity to share in this powerful testimony. They blew it, though, by selling a piece of property and keeping part of the money for themselves. Ananias probably put his devout face on as he handed over a portion of the proceeds—but Peter saw through the masquerade. "Ananias," Peter said, "what made you think of doing such a thing? You have not lied to men but to God."

Ananias and Sapphira were selfish—and they paid with their lives. Likewise, we will pay a great price if we allow materialism to erode our testimony. More than two hundred years ago a professor named Alexander Tytler wrote that the "average age of the world's greatest civilizations has been 200 years." He chronicled their progression through this sequence:

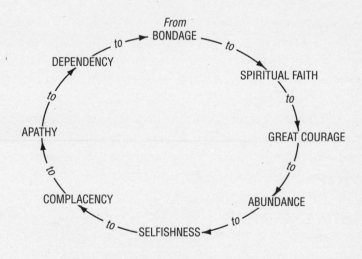

FIGURE 5.1

Given this historical progression of a nation, we must ask ourselves where we, as individuals, are in the cycle. Do we have an abundance? If so, are we generous—or have we allowed selfishness to cloud our thinking? (It doesn't matter whether or not you are a Christian. When you have an abundance, you will always wrestle to some degree with things such as self-ishness, complacency, and apathy.)

The more we have, the harder it is to live by faith—which is why the progression works the way it does. But once we adopt a scriptural perspective on money—that it may be used as a tool, a test, and a testimony—we need to go back to the original question: *Are we using our money the way God wants us to?*

HOW TO HEAR GOD'S SPECIFIC WORD FOR YOU

ANSWERING THIS QUESTION MAY INVOLVE DISCOVER-ING God's specific plan for a particular situation. Sometimes you may wrestle with a needs-versus-wants decision, as my friend Jim did. He wondered whether or not it was right for him to spend so much money on a house. For him, the ability to *afford* the home was not the issue; it was whether or not he should *live* in such a nice home.

At other times you may need to discern God's will regard-ing giving. I remember a time when Judy and I made a finan-cial pledge to a well-known parachurch organization. As the year went by, we found ourselves unable to meet the obliga-tion. I spent time praying about the matter, asking God what we should do about the pledge.

His answer came as I read 2 Corinthians 8:10–11: "Last year you were the first not only to give but also to have the desire to do so. Now finish the work, so that your eager willingness to do it may be matched by your completion of it, according to your means."

I did not know what I could do. The only spare cash we had was in a savings account. The sum was equal to what we owed on the pledge—but it had been earmarked for our family vacation, not for giving. As we read the Bible and prayed, however, Judy and I became convinced we should give the money to the parachurch ministry. Our vacation would just have to wait.

We had planned to take the kids out west to a guest ranch. With five children and five different interest levels and abilities to consider, the ranch seemed like a good idea, and we had all been looking forward to the trip. Putting the vacation on hold, perhaps indefinitely, was no easy decision.

We canceled our reservation. Almost immediately, the fellow who owned the place called back to ask if we would come as his guests. He was willing to foot the bill for all seven of us—including our airfare—if I would conduct a financial seminar for the other guests while we were there. I quickly agreed.

Shortly thereafter, I was asked to speak to a Christian audience on board a cruise ship. The organization sponsoring the cruise invited me to bring the whole family along.

Finally, a family camp located on one of Georgia's most beautiful beaches called to see if I would be willing to speak on the subject of finances at an upcoming retreat. They, too, included our whole family.

All told, we had three unforgettable—and totally paid for—vacations that summer. I can't help but wonder if God would have blessed us so extravagantly had Judy and I refused to fulfill our pledge!

Regardless of the financial questions you face, you need to go back to the decision-making process and start by hearing God's Word. How? For starters, you can read the Bible and pray, as Judy and I did. You can also take sermon notes, recognizing that it is God, and not the pastor, who brings the message to your ears. I try to listen and take notes avidly every Sunday—even when the pastor speaks on a subject such as finances, and I feel certain I know more than he does!

In addition to hearing God's word through Bible reading, prayer, and the church, you can keep a journal to record everything from your questions to God's answers. I've done this for the past twenty years, and I cannot imagine a more powerful or tangible way in which the Lord could make his voice clear to me.

As I read the Bible, I often ask myself three questions about each passage: First, *what does the passage say?* Rephrase the verses in your own words. Next, *what does it mean?* How would you interpret the words as you read them? Finally, *what does the passage say to you, personally?* Ask yourself how you can apply the verses to your daily life. Use your journal to record your answers to these questions so you have a record and a reminder of what the Lord is teaching you.

God is always at work around us, and he is ready to communicate his plan.

God is always at work around us, and he is ready to communicate his plan. Our job is simply to listen—and then to step out in faith and obedience.

GOD OWNS IT ALL

WHEN MY FRIEND JIM BEGAN READING the Bible and praying, his appetite for God's Word became voracious. Sometimes, his wife later told me, he would spend hours a day reading the Bible—and it got so that she could hardly get him to do anything else!

What Jim discovered, among other things, is that God really does own it all. Since his house, ultimately, belonged to God, Jim figured that how he used the home—and whether he kept it or not—was up to the Lord. Jim would obey God, no matter what the Lord said.

God gave Jim the freedom to keep the home. Having heard God's word, Jim became one of the most generous people I know. He, like King David, recognized that everything he had—and everything he gave—belonged to God.

He also pursued the other steps in the generosity process. He identified and handled his financial problems, paying off the house to get out of debt. He developed a perspective on God's work, gladly opening his home for retreats, Bible studies, and other ministry opportunities so that generosity became part of his everyday life. And he had a plan, marking the limits on his lifestyle, so he had money available to give.

In the next chapter I will address the next phase in the generosity process: problem solving. We'll talk about how you can handle your financial problems so that you may give generously in response to God's call. Before you get there, though, take a moment to evaluate your willingness and ability to listen to God. If you are not sure whether or not you are using your money properly right now, then ask him. Get out your Bible, your pen, and a pad or a notebook, and begin by hearing God's word.

Financial problems are the symptoms we see when deeper, more significant issues cloud our thinking. Almost everyone feels a financial pinch at some point—but before we shrug off our problems as commonplace, we need to deal with the underlying causes. We need to change our direction. That change involves four simple—yet powerful—steps.

Problem Solving

Getting a Fix on Your Finances

FRANK SQUEEZED HIS WIFE'S HAND AND SMILED, hoping he looked more confident than he felt. He and Shirley had decided to approach a credit counseling service in an effort to untangle the financial mess they had created. In the process they had divulged almost everything about themselves to a complete stranger, a woman who had access to their paycheck stubs, credit card statements, medical bills, and other intensely personal information. Now, Frank and Shirley awaited her verdict.

"You'll have to declare bankruptcy," the woman said.

Frank looked at Shirley, reading her thoughts. He guessed that she would not willingly accept the bankruptcy option, and he was right. Even as the woman spoke, Shirley's mind raced back to her childhood on a farm in upstate New York. Her father had been a welder, and when the union he belonged to called for a strike, the family would go months at a time with no income. Even so, Shirley's parents had managed to provide for their three daughters. What's more, they always set money aside for the church. Week after week Shirley saw the family's tithe envelope sitting on her mother's bedroom dresser. Giving was a fact of life, as constant and predictable as the morning sunrise. Bankruptcy, on the other hand, was not.

As an adult, Shirley had adopted her parents' financial priorities as her own, tithing regularly even when she found herself divorced, jobless, and with three children of her own to raise. With a mixture of gratitude and awe, she had grown to depend on God, recognizing his faithfulness. Once, when she was out of work and facing some hospital bills, one of her daughters had come home from school with a plain, white envelope in her hand. Shirley's name had been typed on the envelope. Inside, she found a $100 bill. She had no idea where the money came from—which meant she had no choice but humbly to accept and receive God's provision.

Their mutual trust in the Lord was one of the things that had initially attracted Shirley and Frank to one another. As newlyweds, they were eager to use biblical guidelines as they blended their families and their resources, and they envisioned a secure financial future. And why shouldn't they feel optimistic? They both had good jobs and no debt, other than the mortgage on their home.

But then a business deal went sour, and Frank found himself out of a job. He got another one—only to lose it six months later when his employer declared bankruptcy. Frustrated by his pawn-like status in the employment chess game, Frank decided to start his own company, doing kitchen remodeling and other home renovations. Shirley was less than enthused. She knew Frank had a big heart, and she feared his compassionate tendencies would carry too much weight when difficult business decisions had to be made.

Shirley's instincts turned out to be right. The company lost money almost from the start, even when Frank worked seven days a week to get ahead. Shirley's income could not sustain their family—and after a medical emergency landed Frank in the hospital for heart surgery, things went from bad to worse.

Creditors began calling daily, and when they couldn't reach Frank or Shirley, they telephoned their neighbors. Plans were in the works to auction off the couple's home. Never, they told themselves, had they been so humiliated or embarrassed in all their lives.

Even so, they were not prepared to declare bankruptcy. "Isn't there something else we can do?" Shirley asked the credit counselor.

"Well . . ." the woman hesitated. "You owe a lot of money. Your house, your car, your credit cards, your IRS bills—everything is way behind. We could work out some sort of payment schedule, but it will take some time. And," she added, "you certainly don't have enough money to tithe. There comes a time when your church needs to take care of you."

Frank and Shirley could not imagine asking their church for money. After all, they reasoned, their problem was not about putting food on the table. It was about getting out of debt—and that, they knew, was a responsibility they could not shirk.

But the credit counselor had a point. Frank and Shirley were facing a mountain of debt—and no matter how generous they wanted to be, the stark reality was that they simply could not give much until they solved their financial problems. Shirley worked out a compromise in her head.

"We will make the payments according to your schedule," she offered, "but we will also continue to give our tithe. It may not be much, at first—but there will always be someone who has a greater need than we do."

Shirley turned to her husband. "The bottom line is, do we trust God, or don't we?"

They both knew the answer to the question. Their trust in God was the very thing that would see them through the long and difficult road ahead. Resolving to cling to that trust, Frank

and Shirley added up their total debt and gave away one percent of that amount to someone who, they figured, needed the
money even more than they did.

FINANCIAL PROBLEMS: SPOTTING THE SYMPTOMS

DEVASTATING AS THEIR SITUATION WAS, Frank and
Shirley faced a financial picture that is not at all uncommon. I
hear stories like theirs—and worse—all the time. Whether it's
through the excessive use of credit, a poor business decision, or
some totally unforeseen turn of events—such as a costly medical emergency or the sudden loss of a job—many of us will, at
some point, find ourselves in a difficult financial position.

Unlike Frank and Shirley, though, our financial problems
may not appear obvious or even very severe. If we feel the
pinch of insecurity or frustration, we may try to shrug it off,
telling ourselves that *everyone* has bills to pay, kids to raise,
groceries to buy, and cars and houses to pay for. Yet the unease
we feel on the surface may be symptomatic of a deeper, more
significant issue.

**Whether it's through the excessive use of credit, a
poor business decision, or some totally unforeseen
turn of events, many of us will, at some point, find
ourselves in a difficult financial position.**

Certainly there are legitimate reasons for concern. The lat-
est projections on future college costs, for example, are enough
to send shivers up any parent's spine: experts say that eighteen
years from now it will cost at least $100,000 for a four-year

stint at a public college or university. To be able to afford the bill, Mom and Dad are advised to start saving as soon as Baby comes home from the hospital (if not sooner). Assuming an education cost inflation rate of seven percent and a ten percent investment return, parents should invest $170 per month, per child, during each of the eighteen years between the cradle and college. (And that's just to pay for a public institution; if you have your heart set on a private university, plan to increase your college savings rate to about $440 per month for each child!)

And then there's retirement. Do you think you can afford it? Even the very wealthiest Americans—those with incomes topping the $200,000-a-year mark—worry that they won't have enough money to retire on, once inflation eats into their savings.[1] What about you? Are you saving enough? Many of today's investors—especially younger baby boomers—have never felt the pinch of a major market crash or a long bear market. They think that because their investments earned a lot last year, they will continue to provide high returns. As a result, they tend to undersave. In fact, some experts estimate that baby boomers are saving only *a third* of what they actually need to save for retirement.

If you are not sure about the adequacy of your plans for the future, the worksheet in figure 6.1 can help you determine how much you need to be saving for retirement.

College costs, retirement needs, and other big-ticket items can generate the frustration and anxiety associated with hidden financial problems. So can debt. Owing money, in and of itself, is not necessarily a problem—but if indebtedness is a source of tension or uncertainty in your life, stop and ask yourself a few questions. *Do you know how much you owe? Do you have a realistic repayment plan? Month by month, are you climb-*

ing out of debt—or are you getting in deeper and deeper? The
frustration you sense as you try to make ends meet, or the anxiety you feel when the monthly notices arrive, may be symptomatic of an underlying need to reevaluate your spending
habits and get your finances in order.

**The frustration you sense as you try to make ends
meet, or the anxiety you feel when the monthly
notices arrive, may be symptomatic of an
underlying need to reevaluate your spending
habits and get your finances in order.**

While financial frustration and anxiety may clamor for our
attention, an equally telling—yet much quieter—clue to our
secret financial troubles lies in our giving habits. I've asked
countless ministers how many people in their congregations
tithe by giving 10 percent of their income, and the answer is
never more than about 15 percent. What does that mean?
That means that at least 85 percent of us think tithing is
unnecessary, unimportant, or impossible.

If you think you cannot afford to tithe, or you wrestle with
worry and fear over things like college costs, retirement, or
debt, you probably have a financial problem that needs to be
solved. To fail to address it is to invite disaster. To address it
effectively, you need to change your direction.

CHANGING DIRECTIONS

SAY YOU'RE IN KANSAS AND you want to see the Pacific
Ocean. You pack your bags, gas up the car, and grab your

RETIREMENT PLANNING WORKSHEET

STEP BY STEP	EXAMPLE	YOURSELF
1. In today's dollars, enter your best guess as to how much annual income you will need during retirement (suggestion: about 75% of current annual pre-tax income).	$37,500	_____
2. In today's dollars, subtract the amount of annual income you expect to receive from your Social Security benefits. (Contact the social security administration for assistance: 800-772-1213.)	assume -$14,600	_____
3. In today's dollars, subtract the amount of annual income you expect to receive from your pension at work. (Contact your personnel department for assistance.)	assume -$8,132	_____
4. This is the amount of annual income you will need to supply from your personal savings.	= $14,768	_____
5. To allow for the effects of inflation, select the number of years until you retire and enter the factor from the table below. (Table assumes 4% inflation.)	x 2.19	_____

Years Until Retirement	5	10	15	20	25	30	35	40
Factor	1.22	1.48	1.80	2.19	2.67	3.24	3.95	4.80

	EXAMPLE	YOURSELF
This is the approximate amount of income you will need during your first year of retirement to sustain your current standard of living, assuming inflation averages 4% per year.	= $32,342	_____
6. Multiply Item 5 by 16.7. Assuming a more conservative 6% annual return on investments after you retire, this is the amount of capital needed to generate Item 5.	$540,111	_____
7. Enter the amount you've already saved in IRA, company saving plan, fixed or variable annuity, and other tax-deferred accounts.	$57,600	_____
8. To estimate the future value of your current tax-deferred investments, multiply Item 7 times the factor from the table below. (Table assumes 8% return and no taxes.)	x 4.66	_____

Years Until Retirement	5	10	15	20	25	30	35	40
Factor	1.47	2.16	3.17	4.66	6.85	10.06	14.78	21.72

	EXAMPLE	YOURSELF
	= $268,416	_____

Continued on next page

RETIREMENT PLANNING WORKSHEET *continued*

STEP BY STEP	EXAMPLE	YOURSELF
9. Enter the amount you've already saved in taxable accounts such as bank CD's, money markets, mutual funds, and brokerage accounts.	$34,500	_____
10. To estimate the future value of your current taxable investments, multiply Item 9 times the factor from the table below. (Table assumes 8% return and 34% combined fed/state tax bracket.)	x 2.80	_____
Years Until *Retirement* 5 10 15 20 25 30 35 40 *Factor* 1.29 1.67 2.16 2.80 3.62 4.68 6.05 7.83	=$96,600	_____
11. Add items 8 and 10. This is the total estimated value of your current savings when you reach retirement.	$365,016	_____
12. Subtract Item 11 from Item 6. This represents the amount you still need to accumulate before you retire. (If the result is a negative number you have more than you need!)	$175,095	_____
13. Multiply Item 12 times the factor from the table below to get an approximation of the amount you need to add to your tax-deferred savings each year in order to accumulate Item 12 and reach your goal by the time you retire. (Table assumes 8% return and no taxes.)	x .0210	_____
Years Until *Retirement* 5 10 15 20 25 30 35 40 Factor .1639 .0664 .0354 .0210 .0132 .0085 .0056 .0037	=$3,677 per year	_____

FIGURE 6.1 SOURCE: SOUND MIND INVESTING

morning cup of coffee at the drive-thru. Moments later you're on the interstate, breezing along with the day's first rays of sunshine in your eyes.

Sunshine in your eyes? Wait a minute—that's not right! A quick glance at the map confirms your suspicions. You're heading *east*, toward the sunrise. To get to the Pacific you will need to turn around. And the sooner you do it, the better.

That's how it is with our finances. We may have a goal on the horizon, but if we're not headed in the right direction, we'll never get there. And if we don't change our course, we're apt to wind up someplace where we never wanted to go.

It's not *what* you choose to spend your money on, it's *how much* you spend.

Changing your financial direction is a four-step process: *You need to spend less than you earn, avoid debt, build liquidity, and set long-term goals.* To omit even one of these steps is to miss the mark—you might make it to Las Vegas, so to speak, but you'll never get through California to see the ocean.

Spend Less Than You Earn

Most of the people who rely on our firm for financial and investment counsel genuinely want to handle their resources wisely. Many of them, however, make the very same mistake most Americans make—and it's the biggest obstacle there is to financial freedom. It's a *consumptive lifestyle*. By consumptive, I mean a lifestyle in which we spend more than we can

---

We think in terms of what we could do or buy with 100 percent of our income—but after taxes, giving, debt repayment, and savings are taken out, we really have only about 45 to 60 percent left to use.

---

afford to—or more than we should, given our goals and priorities. It's not *what* you choose to spend your money on, it's *how much* you spend.

Why is overspending such a significant problem? Simply put, it's because we have limited resources to use on unlimited alternatives, and living within our income means that tough choices must be made. We think in terms of what we could do or buy with 100 percent of our income—but after taxes, giving, debt repayment, and savings are taken out, we really have only about 45 to 60 percent left to use. Illustrated, our situation might look like this:

Where The Money Goes

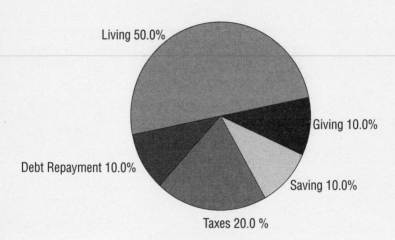

FIGURE 6.2

In order to spend less than we earn (or, as my son Tim puts it, "spend less than your dad earns"), we need to start thinking in terms of how we can use the 45 to 60 percent available to us. These decisions are part of your personal budgeting process. Once we begin living within our means, we create a positive cash flow. A positive cash flow is a critical prerequisite to building liquidity—step three in the direction-changing process—and ultimately achieving our long-term goals.

Of course, as with any worthy endeavor, the decision to spend less than we earn demands *commitment, discipline,* and *time*. To get from the Kansas wheatfields to the California coastline, you must pass exit signs pointing toward any number of interesting sights and attractions. Your *commitment* to seeing the Pacific Ocean is what will keep you from venturing off the highway. At other times, on those long stretches of road when the scenery never changes, you may get tired. You've been driving for what seems like forever; wouldn't it be easier to just turn around and go home? At those moments, *discipline* will carry you forward.

Spending less than you earn is just like the westward road trip. Like roadside attractions, material desires will arise to distract your focus. Like the seemingly featureless highway, the attempt to live within your means can leave you weary or bored. But if you recognize that your goal will take some *time* to achieve, you'll be better equipped—emotionally and mentally—to stay the course.

Avoid the Use of Debt

As I indicated earlier in this chapter, borrowing money is not the problem. Failure to repay it is. Nowhere does the Bible prohibit borrowing—but as Psalm 37:21 says, "The wicked borrow and do not repay."

Borrowing money is not the problem. Failure to repay it is.

Borrowing money is always easier than paying it back. Interest payments and income taxes conspire to make repayment a difficult process. Suppose, for example, you use a credit card to take your family on vacation, or to get some living room furniture, or to buy some fancy electronic equipment. Let's say the tab comes to $2,000—a debt you figure you can afford because you can afford the payments. Other than making monthly payments, you have no real plan for retiring the debt.

At 19.8 percent interest, by making the minimum monthly payments on your card (and assuming you do not charge anything else), it will take you *32 years* to repay the $2,000 debt. Thanks to the interest charges you'll incur during that time, you'll actually wind up spending a total of $10,000. And, thanks to the income tax bite, you'll need to earn about $15,000 just to have the $10,000 you need. *That's $15,000 of your hard-earned money that can't be used for anything else because you have to make the monthly payments!* And by the time you finally get out from under the debt, your $2,000 worth of vacation memories will have faded, your living room couch will be popping its springs, and your once-fancy electronics will be relics that you no longer have any practical use for.

There's no question that debt repayment can be a long and difficult process. My book, *Taming the Money Monster*, offers a detailed analysis of the steps you can take to get out of debt. In a nutshell, you need to (1) stop going into debt, (2) figure out why you went into debt in the first place and solve that problem, (3) set up a workable repayment plan, and (4) hold yourself accountable to someone. Organizations such as Larry Burkett's Christian Financial Concepts (800-722-1976), or the Consumer Credit Counseling Service (800-388-CCCS), and others can work with you and your creditors to create a repayment plan and ensure that you stick with it.

Build Liquidity

The Girl Scouts have a motto we need to adopt: *Be Prepared.* When the unexpected occurs, it pays to be ready. When you spend less than you earn and build a margin of savings into your budget, you'll have the financial fortitude to meet whatever comes your way. A medical emergency, an expensive car repair, or even the loss of a job will not threaten your financial security.

Likewise, when you build liquidity you have the freedom and flexibility to take advantage of life's opportunities. Setting up a 401(k) retirement account, investing in the stock market, or even buying a new house or a car all become possibilities when you have a cash reserve—and when you have the money in hand, you'll be equipped to make wiser, less pressured, financial decisions.

Let's review. When you spend less than you earn, you create a positive cash flow. When you avoid debt, you free up your future income so you can use it on something other than repayment. Together, these two steps generate liquidity: the tangible resources you need to secure your financial position and take advantage of the opportunities that come your way.

Now what?

Set Long-Term Goals

Goals are the things that provide direction in your life— just as a desire to see the Pacific Ocean dictates that you have to head west. Goals are the philosophical underpinnings of your actions; they are why you do what you do.

As you set goals, remember that the longer-term your perspective is, the better your current decisions will be. Living in Atlanta, we were privileged to be part of the city that hosted the 1996 Summer Olympics. I marveled at the planning that went into the event. A giant timeclock hung over the interstate, counting down the days until the world would arrive on our doorstep. As time passed, the Atlanta Committee for the Olympic Games handled everything—inviting athletes, selling tickets, drafting new transit routes, and even planting shade trees and designing water fountains to provide relief from the city's sweltering summer temperatures.

Just as goals can motivate you to stay the course as you spend less than you earn, avoid debt, and build liquidity, they will dictate how you use your resources once you have them.

It was an amazing feat, eclipsed only by the accomplishments of the athletes themselves. In the months prior to the start of the games, we watched athletes from all over the world running or cycling through Atlanta's streets, tackling the hills over and over again. As I saw their speed and stamina, I could only imagine the conditioning and competition that had brought them to the Olympics. Think about spending four to eight years training for a race that would take just fifty seconds to complete!

Yet if you want to win a gold medal, that's how it is. You can't set your goal a week before the competition begins; you'd be doomed to failure if you did. Likewise, if you want to send your kids to college, you need to start working toward that goal years in advance. If you take a short-term perspective, waiting until your college-bound child is a junior in high school, you may never be able to afford the tuition payments. Extend your time horizon, though, and a whole lot more becomes realistically possible.

So what are your long-term goals? In addition to funding your children's education, you might want to set yourself up for a comfortable retirement or provide for the special needs of one of your relatives. Maybe you want to pay off your mortgage, or purchase a larger home. Perhaps—and I hope this will be the case by the time you finish this book—you want to increase your giving.

Regardless of what they are, your goals must be measurable. Sit down and make a list of your goals. Quantify each one in terms you can measure, and set a date by which it should be accomplished. Then, make a habit of reviewing your goals on a regular basis. They are not destinations in and of themselves; instead, they are the signposts, the markers, on your way to financial freedom. They are your cross-country map.

To solve your financial problems—to eliminate anxiety, to get out of debt, to be able to give more—you need to go through each of the four steps: Spend less than you earn, avoid debt, build liquidity, and set goals. My book, *Master Your Money*, offers strategies, worksheets, and more information to take you through the process, if you need help. For example, if you don't have a budget (or if you have one and it isn't working), *Master Your Money* can show you how to figure out how much you need to live on, and how to allocate your resources to create a positive cash flow.

FINDING A LIFE OF FREEDOM

WHEN FRANK AND SHIRLEY WALKED OUT of the counselor's office, they had an action plan they could follow. They defined their debt, identifying what caused it and taking steps—like cutting up their credit cards—to remedy the situation. They set up a budget. They established long-term goals, and they held themselves accountable to their credit counselor.

On paper, such an action plan might look easy to implement. In reality, though, Frank and Shirley faced a monumental challenge. Their victory over indebtedness demanded discipline, sacrifice, and the willingness to make tough decisions—such as when Frank gave up his own renovation business to work, instead, as a kitchen designer for a large corporation. Trading in his entrepreneurial spirit for new corporate hierarchies and management styles was a difficult emotional adjustment. But Frank recognized the value—and the necessity, even—of steady income, corporate benefits, and stability as he and Shirley regained their financial footing.

All told, it took Frank and Shirley more than three years to solve their financial problems. Through it all, though, they managed to make giving a priority, even when their future looked hopeless. When Shirley asked the question, "Do we really trust God—or don't we?" she knew what Frank would say. Despite their difficulties, they had seen God intervene in their lives too many times to doubt his faithfulness.

Frank and Shirley's trust in God's faithfulness turned out to be well founded. During their problem-solving journey to responsible stewardship, they saw debt forgiven, interest and tax penalties abated, and three refund checks arrive from the IRS! There were several anxious moments as Frank experienced five expensive medical procedures and Shirley underwent two shoulder surgeries; however, all of their medical bills—in addition to their original debt—were paid by the end of the three-year process.

Frank's corporate job turned out to be a comfortable fit for him, and it provided excellent medical coverage. He still designs kitchens, while Shirley works in fundraising for a Christian parachurch organization. She does not see her job as simply asking people for money; instead, she views herself as an "investment counselor" for God's kingdom. And she practices what she preaches, giving generously to her church and other ministries.

Frank and Shirley admit that none of this would be possible had they failed to address their financial problems. If you are wrestling with indebtedness, anxiety, or some other financial concern, ask yourself the same question Shirley did: "Do you trust God, or don't you?" If your answer is yes, then take the steps outlined in this chapter to target and solve your financial problems so you can get on with God's plan for your life.

In chapter 5, we saw the importance of listening to God to prepare ourselves for generous living. Here, we have seen how to change our direction by solving our financial problems. As Shirley and Frank discovered, this process is as dynamic as it is time-consuming: over time, fresh problems will arise to demand solutions, and you will need to plan and replan, solve and resolve.

At the same time, you can move forward in the giving process. In the coming chapter we'll learn how to get God's perspective on giving so that our vision aligns with his purposes for our lives. And then finally, in chapter 8, we'll find out how to translate that vision into action as we chart a strategic course toward generosity.

To be joyful and generous, you have to see things as God sees them. When your beliefs, your vision, and your actions align with his perspective, the results will be nothing short of incredible.

seven

The Right Perspective
Seeing Things As God Sees Them

As I WAS PREPARING TO WRITE THIS CHAPTER, I happened to notice an interesting statistic in *USA Today*. It seems that 38 percent of Americans ages 18 to 29 would be willing to sacrifice happiness for a higher-paying job. The older we get, the less likely we would be to make the swap, but even among folks in the 50- to 64-year-old category, 25 percent say they'd trade happiness for money.[1]

I can't say that this report surprised me all that much, but I had to marvel, nonetheless, at our national perspective. Our perspective determines our beliefs, our vision, our faith, and, ultimately, our actions.

I want to challenge you to see things as they really are. I want you, in other words, to adopt the right perspective. The reason this step is so critical is that many people choose this point to get bogged down in the generosity process. Fresh from focusing on their financial problems, they tend—like folks in the *USA Today* report—to see money as the answer to everything:

If only we had some extra cash, we could take that vacation we need so much . . .

If only Jim would get a raise, then we could pay off the credit cards or set something aside for the kids' college education . . .

If only we could afford a bigger house . . .
If only . . .

If phrases like these define your perspective, let me introduce you to a couple I know. They have no shortage of material wealth—as is evidenced by all the things they own. Their names, in fact, are Mr. and Mrs. Thing:

> Mr. and Mrs. Thing are a very pleasant and successful couple.
>
> At least, that's the verdict of most people who tend to measure success with a "thingometer."
>
> When the "thingometer" is put to work in the life of Mr. and Mrs. Thing, the result is startling.
>
> There is Mr. Thing sitting down on a luxurious and very expensive thing, almost hidden by a large number of other things.
>
> Things to sit on, things to sit at, things to cook on, things to eat from, all shiny and new.
>
> Things, things, things.
>
> Things to clean with and things to wash with and things to clean and things to wash.
>
> And things to amuse, and things to give pleasure and things to watch and things to play.
>
> Things for the long, hot summer and things for the short, cold winter.
>
> Things for the big thing in which they live and things for the garden and things for the lounge and things for the kitchen and things for the bedroom.
>
> And things on four wheels and things on two wheels and things to put on top of the four wheels and things to pull behind the four wheels and things to add to the interior of the thing on four wheels.
>
> Things, things, things.

And there in the middle are Mr. and Mrs. Thing,
    smiling and pleased as punch with things, thinking
    of more things to add
    to things.
Secure in their castle of things.

Do they sound familiar? Whenever I talk about Mr. and Mrs. Thing in a public forum, their story always strikes a chord with the audience. Everyone, it seems, knows someone who fits their description. (And all of us, I suspect, see something of ourselves in the couple.)

Mr. and Mrs. Thing may be secure in their castle of things, but that's not the end of their story. Here it is:

Well, I just want you to know that your things can't
    last.
They're going to pass. There's going to be an end to
    them.
Oh, maybe an error in judgment, maybe a temporary
    loss of concentration,
Or maybe you'll just pass them off to the secondhand
    thing dealer.
Or maybe they'll wind up a mass of mangled metal
    being towed off to the thing yard.
And what about the things in your house?
Well, it's time for bed.
Put out the cat, make sure you lock the door so some
    thing-taker doesn't come and take your things.
And that's the way life goes, doesn't it?
And someday, when you die, they only put one thing in
    the box.
You.

                              —Anonymous

Like the old adage says, "You can't take it with you." Mr. and Mrs. Thing illustrate what it means to have the wrong perspective. Their "thingometer" was quite useless when it came to measuring the value of anything that is truly important. Mr. and Mrs. Thing have a temporal, worldly perspective.

CHALLENGE YOUR PERSPECTIVE: CHANGE YOUR BELIEFS

IF MR. AND MRS. THING ARE the consummate example of temporal thinking, the apostle Paul paints a superb contrast as he shares his view of life. Viewed in light of the highest social and religious standards of his day, Paul carried a flawless pedigree. An Israelite from the elite tribe of Benjamin, he was a strict (and powerful) defender of God's law. Yet while society fussed over his impressive credentials, Paul saw them as worthless: "I consider everything a loss compared to the surpassing greatness of knowing Christ Jesus my Lord, for whose sake I have lost all things," he wrote in Philippians 3:8. "I consider them rubbish, that I may gain Christ."

What do you think Mr. and Mrs. Thing would say if you told them that all their good stuff was basically trash? Probably the same thing Paul's Pharisee friends did when he blasted away at all the things they held dear. But when Paul became a Christian and began to see things from God's perspective, he knew his belief system had to change. No longer could he focus on what he called the "inferior brand of righteousness that comes from keeping a list of rules." Instead, he embraced the "robust kind that comes from trusting Christ—*God's* righteousness" (v. 9 *The Message*). Paul traded his temporal outlook for an eternal perspective.

An interesting corollary to the transformation in Paul's perspective is that it did not become *bigger*, it became *differ-*

ent. Paul could have stayed in his Pharisaic rut, striving for more and more rule-keeping and meticulous attempts at purity. He could have, like Mr. and Mrs. Thing, kept on adding to all that he already possessed, hoping against hope that the accumulation would somehow bring satisfaction and fulfillment. He would have been disappointed, of course, but he certainly would have won plenty of praise from his fellow Israelites in the process.

Society looks on in admiration at people like Mr. and Mrs. Thing, who sit "secure in their castle of things." But that's not God's perspective. If you want to get God's perspective (and if you want to be generous, you'll need it), you have to stop thinking of the here and now and start thinking long-term. You have to focus on eternity. That small change, in and of itself, can have a powerful impact on your vision.

CHALLENGE YOUR PERSPECTIVE: CHANGE YOUR VISION

I LIKE VISIONARY PEOPLE. I like reading about them, meeting them, and getting to know them in a way that lets me catch their vision, too. Visionary people don't always see how, and they don't always know when, but they can see the end result—and they can describe it in real-life, real-world terms.

Bill Gates is one of today's most trumpeted visionaries. Back when he launched the Microsoft Corporation, computers seemed more akin to the stuff of science fiction novels than the ubiquitous presence they are in offices and homes today. But Gates found a way to introduce us to the power, possibilities, and ease of personal computing. He communicated his vision and showed us how to make it real—and today Gates ranks as one of the world's wealthiest men.

Another visionary, Bill Johnson, noticed the Ritz-Carlton hotels when there were only three or four in existence. He bought the Ritz-Carlton name and one hotel—an investment that no doubt raised a few eyebrows among the more skeptical entrepreneurs. Yet Johnson could see what other investors could not: a worldwide chain of luxury hotels that are now almost priceless.

Madeleine Albright is a visionary of another sort. Raised in poverty in war-torn Europe, she rose to become Secretary of State under President Bill Clinton. As I write this, she has only held her post for a few months, yet already she has managed to communicate her vision for the United States as a powerful world leader. So far, she has implemented her vision in a diplomatic context around the world, and, according to media polls, she has succeeded in drawing support from the American public as she explains not just the specific policies, but *why* they are important to the future of America and the world. Only time will prove the strength of Secretary Albright's successes; from this vantage point, however, she appears to be a woman of considerable foresight.

Gates, Johnson, and Albright have used their vision to shape the future of technology, business, and politics. Today, some in God's kingdom have launched incredibly powerful initiatives of another kind—initiatives undertaken as a result of a vision grounded in eternity. Bill McCartney, the founder of Promise Keepers, is one of these people.

I serve on the Board of Directors for Promise Keepers, and I've come to value Bill McCartney's friendship as well as his leadership ability. He takes no personal credit for the phenomenal growth of the Promise Keepers movement; rather, he points to his God-given vision as the reason for its success. And what a vision it is! When McCartney organized the first Promise Keepers meeting in 1991, twenty-two men showed up. They may not have been many in number, but they were all committed to each other and to the leadership of Jesus Christ.

McCartney knew that was just the beginning. In his mind's eye, he could see entire stadiums filled with like-minded men—yet who would have believed that at the first gathering? Who would have thought that in Atlanta we'd see more than 68,000 men turn out for two days of teaching, worship, and fellowship in a stadium that was sold out months in advance? I had the privilege of speaking to the group one afternoon. Standing before so many men who were serious about their families and their faith was a moving, unforgettable experience!

As I write this, the Promise Keepers organization looks toward an upcoming conference in Washington, D.C., where a racially and denominationally diverse group of one million men will pray for revival and repentence in America in obedience to God's commands (see 2 Chron. 7:14). By the time this book hits the stores, three or four million men will have participated in a Promise Keepers conference. Three or four million men—where there were once only twenty-two. Who could have seen it? Only someone with an eternal perspective.

Like Bill McCartney, Bill Bright has an eternity-based vision that almost defies comprehension. The founder of Campus Crusade for Christ, Dr. Bright has devoted his life to the fulfillment of the Great Commission, and he believes it can happen by the year 2000.

When I first met Dr. Bright twenty-two years ago, I was a brand-new Christian. Back then, I didn't really understand what he was talking about when he shared his vision to reach the world for Christ. Later, when I began to grasp his meaning, I thought he was a little crazy. But now, with the new millennium practically upon us, I can see his vision becoming a reality. I believe it really could happen.

Dr. Bright's plan, called New Life 2000, has a multitude of components, ranging from door-to-door evangelism to mass showings of the *Jesus* film, which more than one billion people have seen so far. A key part of the New Life 2000 strategy is to divide the world's six billion people into five thousand segments of one million people each, defined by a common characteristic such as culture or geography. Each of these five thousand groups can then be analyzed and targeted with remarkable precision and efficiency.

As I look around today, I see Christians who have a vision that they cannot communicate. Even more than that, I see Christians—and entire churches— who exist without any compelling vision at all.

This awesome undertaking is already well on its way. Ralph Winters, head of the U.S. Center for World Missions, has endorsed New Life 2000 as the only world evangelism plan in existence that has any legitimacy, thanks to the program's strategy, resources, and ability to monitor and measure its results.

Why did God use Bill Bright to launch this initiative? I believe it is because Dr. Bright sees the Spirit of God moving in ways that the rest of us don't see or cannot comprehend. He has a willingness to see things as God sees them. He sees things, in other words, as they really are.

As I said earlier, one mark of an effective visionary is the ability to describe the outcome of a vision in real-life terms. As I look around today, I see Christians who have a vision that they cannot communicate. Even more than that, I see Christians—and entire churches—who exist without any compelling vision at all.

Most of us, I am afraid, are like the ten spies who went up with Joshua and Caleb to scout out the Promised Land. Remember that story? There the Israelites were, camped out in the desert and grumbling about the food. At God's command, Moses sent a delegation of twelve men into Canaan to scout out the land God had promised to give them. The spies pulled off a thorough reconnaissance mission, even bringing back some fruit—a single cluster of grapes that had to be carried by two men—as evidence of their findings.

As to the beauty and lushness of the land, the twelve were unanimous. "It flows with milk and honey!" they said. But there was more to tell: The inhabitants of the land were giants. "We can't attack these people," the spies said. "They are stronger than we are. In fact, we looked like grasshoppers by comparison!"

At this, the Israelites began to howl and bemoan their fate. But Caleb, one of the twelve who took the Canaan tour, silenced the crowd. "We should go up and take possession of the land," he charged, "for we can certainly do it."

Caleb—along with another spy named Joshua—saw things from God's perspective, as they really were. By contrast, the other ten spies left God out of the equation entirely, taking in the sights with a fear and hopelessness born out of their temporal, worldly vision. No wonder they saw the task of overtaking Canaan as impossible.

If yours is an eternal perspective—if you see things as God sees them—then watch for the vision God will give you. When he does, remember the principle that Joshua and Caleb no doubt understood: When you do your part and God does his part, anything and everything is possible.

CHALLENGE YOUR PERSPECTIVE: CHANGE YOUR FAITH

HEBREWS 11 HAS BEEN CALLED the Bible's "Hall of Faith." Faith, as I see it, is how you respond to what you know (your beliefs) and what you see (your vision). Once your beliefs and your vision line up with God's perspective, the results will be nothing short of incredible.

Consider just a few of the folks who made it into the Hall of Faith: Abraham, who left his homeland because he could see a heavenly city with real, eternal foundations; Sarah, Abraham's ninety-year-old wife who heard God speak and then became pregnant because she believed his seemingly impossible promise. And Noah, who built a giant ship in the middle of dry land because God had told him of the coming flood. Some theologians maintain that nobody had ever even seen rain in Noah's day and that the crops were watered by mists and underground springs—yet Noah obeyed God because of his faith. He—like Abraham, Sarah, and the rest of the heroes in Hebrews—used his beliefs and his vision to inspire obedient action.

> **If we have the eternal perspective to see things as they really are, we cannot rest on our beliefs or our vision. We have got to get moving. We have got to exercise our faith.**

In a sense, I can identify with these people. In 1979, when God called me to start our firm, I envisioned thousands and thousands of people managing their financial resources according to biblical principles. I believed that if they did this, they would be eager and able to give more—and I saw billions of dollars being made available for fulfilling the Great Commission. To some, it may have been a far-fetched dream—yet to me it was real. Armed with the beliefs and the vision God had given me, I stepped out in faith and launched the company.

Henry Blackaby, the author of *Experiencing God*, says we should attempt things so great that they are doomed to failure unless God intervenes.[2] To attempt demands action. If we have the eternal perspective to see things as they really are, we cannot rest on our beliefs or our vision. We have got to get moving. We have got to exercise our faith.

What would have happened had Abraham believed God and envisioned the eternal city—yet refused to uproot his family to embark on such an arduous journey? What would have happened if the Israelites had listened to Joshua and Caleb—yet stayed camped where they were, to be on the "safe" side? And what would have happened had Bill Bright recognized the possibilities of a program like New Life 2000—and then kept the vision locked in his heart where no one could scoff at it?

In each of these cases, of course, God could have called someone else or shifted gears in the plan; he is, after all, the sovereign ruler of the universe. Yet Abraham, the Israelites, Bill Bright, and countless others would have missed the opportunity to be part of God's grand design. They would have had the beliefs and the vision—but without faith, they would have missed the blessing.

GETTING IN ON THE BLESSING

WHAT ABOUT YOU? DO YOU HAVE a God-given vision? Are you actively responding to that vision in faith? Is God using you in a way you can measure? Are you getting in on his blessing?

If not, I want to challenge you to examine your perspective. In order to see things as they really are, start by anchoring your beliefs and your vision in the reality of what God is doing in the world around you. Earlier in this chapter, I said I like being with visionary people. One of the significant benefits I get from serving on the boards for Promise Keepers, Campus Crusade, and other Christian organizations is the chance to see and hear what's going on in the world and how God is working.

You can do the very same thing right where you are. If your church has a youth group, for example, find out if they have a summer outreach program and tap into what's going on there. If you're not already doing so, get on the mailing lists of the missionaries you know and then take an active part in praying for the needs they outline in their letters. Take a short-term missions trip yourself. Such "vision trips," as I call them, are probably the best way I know to find out, firsthand, what God is doing and how you can get in on it.

Proverbs 29:18 (KJV) says, "Where there is no vision, the people perish." This, then, is why I believe we are at a critical stage in the generosity process. You may hear God's Word and solve your financial problems, but without the right perspective—God's perspective—you will not be able to go on.

LEARN TO RECEIVE SO YOU CAN GIVE

HAVING THE BELIEFS, THE VISION, and the faith that come from an eternal perspective will enable you to move forward. Taken together with the first two steps in the process—the preparation and the problem solving—they will propel you into the final phase of the generosity cycle: *the plan*.

In the next chapter, you'll meet a man who developed and followed a financial plan for giving. When you read his story—

which is as motivating as it is remarkable—you may feel intimidated, at first, by his commitment to generous living. But there's an interesting twist to his tale. In order to be generous, this man had to learn to receive. He never would have achieved his giving goals had he not been willing to recognize and accept God's provision for his material needs.

Frank and Shirley, the couple you read about in chapter 5, faced the same hurdle. Back when Shirley's daughter brought home that hundred-dollar bill, Shirley admits she would have tried to return the money had she known who had given it to her. For them—and for so many of us—learning to receive can be just as difficult (if not more so) than learning to give.

"Listen carefully to what I am saying—and be wary of the shrewd advice that tells you how to get ahead in the world on your own. Giving, not getting, is the way. Generosity begets generosity. Stinginess impoverishes."

In the coming chapter you'll discover how to formulate a practical plan for giving. If your giving goals seem loftier than you think you can realistically achieve, take a moment to evaluate your willingness to receive. When a friend wants to pay for your dinner, or someone gives you their hand-me-down clothes, or your in-laws offer to help you buy a new family car, *could it be that God is using these people to provide for your material needs? Could it be that he wants to free you up, financially, so you can give as generously as you'd like to?*

So far, you've learned how to hear God's Word, solve your financial problems, and adopt the perspective you need for

generous living. In order to seal the deal—in order to trans-
form your heart and generate an inner desire to be generous—
you need to start giving. I like the way Jesus puts it in Mark 4
(*The Message*): "Listen carefully to what I am saying—and be
wary of the shrewd advice that tells you how to get ahead in
the world on your own. Giving, not getting, is the way. Generosity begets generosity. Stinginess impoverishes."

Would you be generous—or stingy? Would you be a
giver—or would you be impoverished? If your aim is to be
generous, then read on. If you are ready to give, I am ready to
show you how.

How much is enough? Deciding how much money you need to make or to have is a function of your lifestyle and the "finish lines" you put on the way you want to live. Deciding how much to give, on the other hand, requires an understanding of three basic generosity levels: how much you should give, how much you could give, and how much you would give.

eight

The Plan

How Generous Do You Want to Be?

THINK BACK TO YOUR LAST VACATION. BEFORE YOU left, you needed to make many decisions. First you had to choose your destination: The beach? The mountains? Grandma's house? Did you want to visit someplace comfortable and familiar—or exotic and adventuresome? Perhaps you browsed through your bookstore's "guidebook" section or clipped travel articles out of the newspaper. Maybe you talked to friends, contacted a travel agent, or wrote away for brochures on accommodations and area attractions.

Once you picked the spot, you had to figure out how to get there. Would you drive or fly? Take the highway or the scenic route? Stop for lunch or pack a picnic to eat in the car?

Finally, you had to decide what to pack.

And through it all there were dozens of little details to attend to: Who would take care of your pets and water your plants? Should you arrange for the post office to hold your mail or get a neighbor to pick it up? How much cash should you carry—and should you take some of it in travelers' checks? Should you leave a light on in the living room?

My point in all of this is that vacations don't just "happen." Most people don't suddenly drop what they're doing and head to the airport, figuring they'll pick a destination from the "Departures" menu offered on the overhead monitors. Instead, most vacations require forethought, planning, and days—or even weeks—of preparation.

Likewise, you wouldn't build a home—or anything else, for that matter—without first considering everything from the projected cost to the amount of living space your family needs. Our church recently completed a new building. It's attractive, functional, and architecturally well-suited, to the other structures on the property. It's also paid for. But it didn't just appear one Sunday. This building took years to construct—years that involved saving money, studying blueprints, and holding fast to our vision while the construction crews went about making our dream a reality.

Before you start shooting for the stars in an effort to capture the spirit of generous living, keep your feet on the ground and figure out where you are.

Whether you are planning a vacation, building a church, or picking out a new car, chances are good that you'll spend a significant block of time weighing your options and making your plans—much more time, in fact, than you'd probably spend thinking about charitable giving. Most of us don't plan to give; instead, we give haphazardly—such as when we hear a particularly poignant appeal or when tax time rolls around and we want a tax deduction. As a result, most of us don't give anywhere close to the amount that we could afford—and would honestly like—to give.

Anyone who's tried to navigate an unfamiliar city or town knows the value of a good road map. But imagine being lost, not knowing where you are, with no road markers or signposts on hand to pinpoint your location. Under that scenario, even the most accurate map would be totally useless. When you don't know where you are to begin with, a map is a worthless tool.

The same thing might be said of a plan for giving. If you don't know where you are right now, even the most expertly crafted giving strategy will be wasted. So before you start shooting for the stars in an effort to capture the spirit of generous living, keep your feet on the ground and figure out where you are. Pull out your old tax returns. How much did you give last year? What about the year before that?

Knowing how much you currently give is the first step in designing your own giving plan. Next, you need to figure out where you want to go—or how much, in other words, you want to give. Once you know where you are and where you want to go, simple logic—like a good road map—will tell you how to get there.

This chapter is about discovering where you want to go. It's about setting goals and reaching them. It's about translating your vision into action, keeping in mind the lesson from Mark 4: Generosity begets generosity, while stinginess impoverishes.

One Couple's Story

JACK AND LISA HAVE BEEN MARRIED for nearly sixteen years. When they bought their first home in 1985, the real estate agent who sold it to them figured it wouldn't be long before the $71,000 house would be on the market again. She knew Jack was a doctor, fresh out of medical school—and she reasoned that he would want to upgrade to a larger home in a fancier neighborhood within two or three years. She didn't know any young professionals who would live in such a modest little home—but then, she didn't really know Jack and Lisa.

Throughout med school and his subsequent residency, Jack had seen other doctors pursue wealth and prestige, usually at the expense of their families. Many had wrecked their homes as they concentrated on their careers, and Jack wanted no part of that life. Instead, he felt compelled to reach for something more—and, as he read his Bible, he unconsciously found himself at the start of the generosity process, the preparation phase. He could not escape the power of Luke 6:38: "Give, and it will be given to you," the verse promised. "For with the measure you use, it will be measured to you."

As Jack's medical practice grew, that verse replayed itself over and over again in his mind. "Maybe," he confided to Lisa, "the extra money I'm making is not meant for us. Maybe God is increasing my income so we'll have more money to give away."

Jack had an eternal perspective. He understood the basic truths we covered in chapter 4, including that God owns it all. As a result of their convictions, he and Lisa made a remarkable decision. They set a cap on the lifestyle they wanted to attain. They resolved not to move the markers as their income rose; instead, they planned to use the extra—their cash margin—for strategic "investing": giving to God's kingdom.

Right away, the couple recognized the financial implications their decision would have. They knew they could not, for example, always follow their friends as they moved into larger homes. Instead, the couple stayed in their three-bedroom house for seven years—despite the increasingly crowded conditions as the first four of their five children were born. "It was cramped," Jack admits, "but the kids learned a lot about how to share space."

Likewise, their self-imposed lifestyle cap meant that every spending decision had to be made with the big picture—the eternal perspective—in mind. As Jack continued to drive the Buick sedan he had bought from his mother during medical school, his friends and colleagues must have wondered at his priorities. Why would a doctor drive such an old car? Why didn't Jack and Lisa take many vacations or live in a fancier home? And why, they might have asked (had they known), would anyone walk around with holes in his shoes when he could easily afford to buy a new pair?

The matter of his shoes taught Jack an important lesson. Making his rounds at the hospital, Jack was on his feet almost constantly. He had to wear costly orthopedic shoes—and he knew that to replace them when they began to wear out would leave that much less for him and Lisa to give away. One day, as Jack knelt at the bedside of a young patient, the boy's father noticed the holes in the doctor's shoes. "Please," the man asked, "allow me the privilege of putting new soles on your shoes. It's my business—and I want to thank you for the care you have given my son."

God has a way of providing for our material needs to free up more money for giving.

Jack recognized the man's offer for what it was: God's way of providing for his material needs in order to free up more money for giving. He accepted the man's proposition—and from that day on he took his worn out shoes to his friend whenever they needed repairing.

Over the years, Jack and Lisa's willingness to receive God's provision became a critical factor in their ability to live within the parameters of their chosen lifestyle. Once, when Lisa's parents invited their family to visit them on the west coast, Jack and Lisa felt they had to decline. They were eager to make the trip, but the only way they could afford to fly all seven family members across the country would be to increase their lifestyle spending and cut into their giving budget. It was a difficult decision, but Jack hoped his in-laws would understand why they couldn't accept the invitation.

Lisa's parents understood perfectly. Even so, they were eager to see their grandchildren, so they sent Jack a check to help cover the cost of the trip. Again, Jack saw God's hand at work, and gladly received his blessing.

Stories like these go on and on, as Jack and Lisa recount the times when God met their expenses in ways they had not imagined—from family vacations to the kids' education (which Jack's father unexpectedly offered to help fund). Had they been too proud or unwilling to receive from others, none of these blessings would have come to pass.

Jack and Lisa are real people, and their story is true. By maintaining their lifestyle boundaries, Jack and Lisa were able to steadily increase their giving over the years. Today—even with five children to feed, clothe, and educate—they manage to give away half of everything they earn. But the road has not always been easy. Many times, Jack says, they felt—and still feel—the pinch of sacrifice. Sometimes they battle self-pity or the temptation to increase their living expenses and upgrade their lifestyle. Even so, their commitment to giving has provided them with firsthand exposure to God's promise in Luke 6 (*The Message*): "Give away your life; you'll find life given back, but not merely given back—given back with bonus and blessing."

In effect, what Jack and Lisa did was to set a "finish line" on their lives. This concept is a biblical one: in Hebrews 12 (*The Message*), for example, Paul admonishes us to "Strip down, start running—and never quit! No extra spiritual fat, no parasitic sins. Keep your eyes on *Jesus*, who both began and finished this race we're in. Study how he did it. Because he never lost sight of where he was headed—that exhilarating finish in and with God—he could put up with anything along the way."

If you choose to run life's race with an eternal perspective, that decision will be evidenced by your lifestyle—specifically, how you choose to use the money you have.

Think about where you are headed. Is your focus on eternity? Are you keeping your eyes on Jesus? Or have you allowed the "fat" and "sins" of things such as materialism, covetousness, and self-centeredness to drag you down? If you choose to run life's race with an eternal perspective, that decision will be evidenced by your lifestyle—specifically, how you choose to use the money you have.

SETTING YOUR OWN FINISH LINES

LIKE JACK AND LISA, YOU CAN put a finish line on your lifestyle. With such a cap in place, you can free up more of your cash-flow margin for things that will have lasting value—things such as charitable giving and investing in your family's spiritual growth and development. Financial decisions that might otherwise seem difficult or confusing become natural and easy choices, thanks to your "finish line" focus.

To establish your own finish lines, start by asking yourself some basic questions. What kind of home do you want for your family, and how much will it cost? How much money do you need to meet your living expenses? How much do you need to save—whether it's for college, retirement, or some other long-term goal? How much are you willing to spend on vacations and other leisure activities?

On an athletic track, the finish line serves two purposes. It gives the runners something to aim for, and it signals the stopping point for the athletes who complete the race. In the same manner, financial finish lines help you focus on your goals and keep you from racing past them in pursuit of something else. For example, if your goal is to be out of debt within three years, you might adopt a lifestyle finish line that discourages or prevents additional borrowing. Once your debt is paid off, your finish line will confirm that accomplishment and give you the freedom to divert the funds you had been using for debt repayment to another (more satisfying) use.

I said earlier that Jack and Lisa vowed not to move their finish lines once they began to have more discretionary income. I do not want to leave you with a legalistic picture of a finish line as a barrier that cannot be moved. Instead, let me remind you that we are talking about lifestyle choices. A couple with two children may, for example, envision themselves in a house that costs $100,000. Six years and two more children later, their expanded family may actually wind up buying a more expensive home to get the added space they need. Their living expenses may go up, but their finish line— the type of lifestyle they have chosen for their family— remains constant.

TOUGH CHOICES

AT FIRST GLANCE, DECISIONS relating to living expenses may seem to be strictly economic, the kind of choices you could easily make with the help of a good financial or estate planning book. In reality, though, the answers to these questions will be driven not so much by what you can *afford* to purchase as by what you think you *ought* to buy.

For example, a friend of mine asked whether or not I thought it was all right for him to send his teenage son to a week of soccer camp that cost $1,000. The question was not whether or not my friend could afford to pay for the camp; it was whether or not such an expense was appropriate.

The question we must ask is not "*Can I afford this?*" but "*Would God want me to use his money this way?*"

There is no "right" answer to my friend's question. Instead of looking for a formula or rule to dictate your spending decisions, ask yourself, "What ultimate purpose will this expense fulfill?" If God owns it all, then every spending decision—including $1,000-a-week soccer camps—becomes a spiritual decision. We are always using God's resources. The question we must ask is not "*Can I afford this?*" but "*Would God want me to use his money this way?*"

What would Jack and Lisa say to an expensive soccer camp? If you think they'd immediately dismiss it as a frivolous expense, think again. Just as having an eternal perspective can turn your focus toward giving, it will also open your eyes to the things you can do to develop godly characteristics in your family. Soccer camps may hone athletic skills, but they may also encourage traits such as responsibility, discipline, integrity, and a strong work ethic. Chances are that Jack and Lisa might see a "costly" soccer camp as a very valuable, worthwhile, and economically sound investment in their children's future.

As I mentioned in chapter 2, there will always be needy people. There will always be a "better way," so to speak, to use your money. When you come up against soccer camp questions and other spending decisions, don't fall into the guilt-laden trap of thinking you always have to give your money to the poor, the hungry, and the homeless. Instead, go back to the beginning of the generosity process. Read the Bible and listen to what God is saying. He might want you to give away every cent you have. Or he might want you to send your son to soccer camp. You'll never know unless you ask.

Instead of asking yourself how much money you need and then trying to figure out how much you can give out of whatever's left over, flip-flop your perspective. Start by asking yourself how generous you want to be.

I'll talk more about using our money to provide for our families in chapters 9 and 10. For now, though, I want to focus on how our lifestyle finish lines can affect our giving. When I ask the question, *How much is enough?* most people immediately start thinking about how much money they need to live on, or to save, or to achieve their long-term goals. These considerations are obviously important—especially as you set your lifestyle finish lines—but I want to challenge you to look at the question another way. How much is enough to *give?* Instead of asking yourself how much money you need and then trying to figure out how much you can give out of whatever's left over, flip-flop your perspective. Start by asking yourself how generous you want to be.

THE THREE LEVELS OF GIVING

DECIDING HOW MUCH TO GIVE IS not a function of a set formula; instead, the choice is dependent on three levels: How much you *should* give, how much you *could* give, and how much you *would* give. You can reach any and all of these levels; all it requires is that you make a choice and tackle the three levels in sequential order.

Giving Level	Biblical Description	Amount/ Process	Reason
Should Give	Tithe	Proportionate Ownership	Recognize God's
Could Give	Sacrificial	Planned	Develop Discipline/ Sacrificial Mindset
Would Give	Faith	Pre-committed	Experience a Life of Faith & Joy

FIGURE 8.1

The "Should Give" Level

The "should give" level is the tithe. "Ten percent" is the most commonly used figure today, but in reality, the "tenth" cited in Malachi 3:10 is just one of several giving levels mentioned in the Bible. In the Old Testament, an annual tithe of ten percent was required for the maintenance of the Levites, a second ten percent was used for the Lord's feast, and every third year an additional ten percent was collected for strangers, widows, and orphans (see Lev. 27:30; Num. 18:21; Deut. 14:22). All told, God asked the Israelites to give a whopping twenty-three percent!

In the New Testament's shift from the law to grace, giving guidelines are less specific. Instead of demanding a set percentage or amount, God asks us to give cheerfully and in accordance with how we have been prospered (see 2 Cor. 8:12; 9:6–7). We should give, in other words, in proportion to the amount we have received. For some of us, ten percent may be just the beginning. If we want to give *proportionally*, we may need to give much more than that.

Why does God ask us to give? There are several reasons. The most important reason is that giving acknowledges God's ownership of all of our resources. Giving is a physical, measurable evidence of our belief that God really does "own it all." As Proverbs 3:9–10 points out, giving shows our love for him and our willingness to obey his commands. It acknowledges God as the ultimate provider of everything.

Ecclesiastes 5:15 says, "Naked a man comes from his mother's womb, and as he comes, so he departs." Like Mr. and Mrs. Thing—who had everything money could buy but wound up with just one "thing" in a box—the ultimate reality is that we really do not "own" anything. *Tithing is simply the recognition of ultimate reality.*

How much you give is not so much a reflection of your wealth as it is of your relationship with God.

How much you give, then, is not so much a reflection of your wealth as it is of your relationship with God. You may choose to give a small percentage to acknowledge God's ownership, or you may decide to give it all away. While giving at the "should give" level is a function of your financial position and your understanding of "proportionate" giving, the specific amount you give is, ultimately, a matter between you and the Lord.

Are you comfortable with the amount you are giving? Perhaps, like most American Christians, you currently give away only a small percentage of your income. If you sense the Lord leading you to increase your giving, a few simple guidelines will make the process easier:

First, give *regularly*—1 Corinthians 16:2 says to set aside your gift "on the first day of every week"—and make your giving a *priority*, before you pay your monthly bills.

Next, steadily *increase the amount* as the weeks and months and years go by. You may need to take a hard look at your living expenses to see how you can decrease your spending to meet this objective.

Finally, give yourself *time*. Remember Frank and Shirley? It took them more than three years to reach the giving level they wanted to—but they never gave up and they never stopped giving.

The "Could Give" Level

The "could give" level pertains to sacrificial giving. It's the amount you could give—above and beyond your regular tithe—if you planned and were willing to give up something else. Perhaps you could give more if you postponed your vacation or dipped into your savings account. You might decide not to eat out or go to the movies for a few months so you could have something extra to give, beyond the "should give" level.

The concept of sacrifice is foreign to most American Christians. Most of us would pat ourselves on the back if we consistently reached the ten percent mark, and the idea of giving up vacations, savings accounts, or other lifestyle desires can make us uncomfortable. And in some cases, this "above and beyond" giving is, in fact, almost impossible. Vacations may be only a far-off dream for some of us. Likewise, savings accounts may be non-existent, as month after month every last dollar goes toward housing, food, education, and other basic necessities.

Any time you sacrifice something in order to give—be it money, possessions, time, or something else—you are giving at the "could give" level.

But even if the money is tight, we can still reach the "could give" level. We can sacrifice things like time, talents, and convenience. Every Christian has a "should give" responsibility to serve within the local church, but we can reach the "could give" level by committing volunteer hours "above and beyond" the minimum. One family I know often hosts visiting missionaries in their home, sacrificing space and convenience in an effort to give and live generously. Some people sacrifice time by working with a church outreach program or serving others via a charitable organization. Any time you sacrifice something in order to give—be it money, possessions, time, or something else—you are giving at the "could give" level.

The Bible's classic example of "could give" giving is the story of the poor widow who put only two small coins into the temple treasury. When Jesus saw what she had done, he pointed out the woman to his disciples. "This poor widow has put more into the treasury than all the others," he said. "They all gave out of their wealth; but she, out of her poverty, put in everything—all she had to live on" (Mark 12:43–44). The others, in giving out of their wealth, had reached the "should give" level. But the widow, in giving all she had to live on, practiced sacrificial giving.

Her story is inspiring—and more so when you contrast it with the rich young man Jesus had met just a few days earlier.

That man, who was very wealthy, claimed to have kept all of the commandments. He wondered what else he should do to inherit eternal life.

"'One thing you lack,' [Jesus] said. 'Go, sell everything you have and give to the poor, and you will have treasure in heaven. Then come, follow me'" (Mark 10:21).

The young fellow went away sad. He was not willing to deprive himself of the comfort that characterized his life.

Many of us can identify with the rich young man's reaction. We don't understand or feel easy with small sacrifices; how much more would we shun the idea of giving away all that we have. Yet it is precisely for this reason that God asks us to give. Giving at the "could give" level introduces us to the notion of a sacrificial lifestyle—which, in and of itself, requires that we develop financial discipline.

The "Would Give" Level

Giving at the "could give" level is giving something that can be seen. When you give at this level, you can see the amount, and you know where it will come from (your savings account, a postponed vacation, a scaled-back clothing budget, etc.). When you give at the "would give" level, on the other hand, you give something that cannot be seen. You give by faith.

Unless you precommit to give the surplus, chances are good that when the time comes, you will not give it.

"Would give" giving, or "unseen" giving, happens when you precommit yourself to giving an unexpected surplus that God may provide. (Note: God can do this only if you have a good grasp of your financial picture so that you recognize his provision when it comes either via an increase in income or a decrease in expenses.) Unless you precommit to give the surplus, chances are good that when the time comes, you will not give it. There will always be additional ways to spend the leftovers; as I noted in chapter 3, needs always expand to meet income.

Jack and Lisa's decision to limit their lifestyle and give away the excess catapulted them into the "would give" level. Having crossed the thresholds of acknowledging God's ownership and accepting a sacrificial lifestyle, they began to depend on the Lord to supply their needs. They could not always see where the money would come from to pay for things like vacations and schooling, yet they trusted the Lord and reaped the benefits of his promises. When you give at the "would give" level, you realize the "bonus and blessing" of a life of faith in—and dependency on—God.

Earlier in this chapter I asked you to pull out your old tax returns. Look back at figure 8.1. Which category best describes your current level of giving? At which level would you like to be able to give? Pray about your answers and establish a giving level—either in terms of a specific dollar amount or a percentage of your income—that you believe God wants you to reach.

If you have not been tithing, maybe your goal will be to start giving away four or five percent. If you are already comfortable with the ten-percent tithe mentioned in Scripture and cited by most churches today, perhaps you want to use that level as a springboard to moving into a New Testament level of giving—giving "as God has prospered you."

Regardless of how much we give, we all want our contributions to count. There are so many legitimate needs in the world today; sometimes it can be hard to know where your money will be used most effectively. In the coming chapter, you'll discover how to make wise choices as you learn the secrets of strategic giving—giving that is powerful, effective, and rewarding.

PART three

Practical Applications
for a Generous Life

If God owns everything—and he does—then we are stewards of the resources he gives us. To do our job wisely, we must strive to ensure that our charitable giving is both strategic (effective) and leveraged (efficient). Only then will we be worthy of the Lord's commendation: "Well done, good and faithful servant!"

nine

Strategic Giving

Making Your Charitable Contributions Count

STEVE BECAME A CHRISTIAN TWENTY YEARS AGO, but he remembers the transformation as though it happened yesterday. All the teachings of the Bible seemed fresh and new, including the parts about tithing and fulfilling the Great Commission. Steve had always given token amounts to his church and to various social causes, but suddenly he wanted to do more. He was ready and eager to "evangelize the world."

Where he had once given sparingly, Steve began a torrent of generosity. He threw open the floodgates, both in his personal finances and through his company, giving hundreds (and sometimes thousands) to almost anyone who asked: churches, schools, and all manner of charitable organizations. Steve knew God wanted Christians to give—and he, for one, was not about to hold anything back.

Steve began getting calls at home—fundraising appeals that, for the most part, he readily welcomed. After all, he wanted to be generous, didn't he? Focused as he was on winning others to Christ, all Steve asked the callers was whether or not they "knew Jesus."

"Oh yes," the solicitors answered. "Just send us five hundred dollars. That will really help."

After a while, Steve began to get suspicious. The calls he received followed a certain pattern, with a fundraising pitch that became more familiar with each successive call. In his zeal to write and mail the checks, Steve had never thought to inquire as to how the funds would be used or where the money was actually going. He decided to do a little detective work.

Steve began by asking callers to identify themselves and provide information about the organization or ministry they represented. Some callers made feeble attempts to legitimize themselves; others simply hung up when Steve pressed for more details. Eventually, the solicitations stopped altogether.

Steve realized that he had been had. Emboldened by their initial success, a group of phoney telemarketers had pegged him as an "easy sell," calling him time after time with several different—yet all seemingly worthy—appeals. Steve later learned of a telemarketing ring that operated out of a single hotel room not far from where he lived, and he suspected that he had been targeted by that group.

We are responsible for managing God's resources.

Embarrassed as he was by his gullibility, Steve did not give up on giving; instead, he resolved to change his perspective. Instead of simply doling out money in a blind desire to be generous, Steve began to see giving as something to be done responsibly and with care. Steve began to learn about "stewardship."

The dictionary defines a *steward* as "a person who manages another's property or financial affairs." If God owns everything we have, then we are his stewards. We are responsible for managing God's resources.

Today, about 80 percent of the world's evangelical dollars—the money used for evangelism—is in North America. American Christians, therefore, have an awesome responsibility. Not only must we avoid fraudulent and deceptive organizations like the telemarketers who targeted Steve, we must also choose from among an overwhelming array of legitimate and worthy appeals. God does not ask us to meet every need—that's a job he reserves for himself. Instead, he wants us to give wisely. As a friend of mine put it, "I once thought it didn't matter where I gave, as long as I gave from the heart. Now I know God expects me to be a good steward of his money."

Wise stewardship is what this chapter is all about. While the principles we'll cover are couched in financial terms, the lessons are equally applicable to the way you use all the resources God gives you. In chapter 4, we discussed generosity as a lifestyle with practical applications for your home, your workplace, and your community. Wherever you are, and whether your focus is on giving money, talents, or time, you want your contributions to be both effective and efficient. You want your gifts, in other words, to be *strategic* and *leveraged*.

STRATEGIC GIVING

STORIES LIKE STEVE'S MIGHT SEEM ALMOST laughable, were they not so common. Hugh Maclellan, who serves on our firm's Board of Directors, heads up one of the country's largest Christian charitable organizations. In his estimation, fully half of all giving is ineffective. "Most people," he says, "give in response to emotional or persistent appeals. Very few

of us take the time to check out an organization to see whether
the need is justified or whether the group can produce results."

**Most people give in response to emotional or
persistent appeals. Very few of us take the time to
check out an organization to see whether the need is
justified or whether the group can produce results.**

Hugh's perspective might be used as a definition for "effective" giving. Before you give to an individual, a church, or a
ministry, check it out. Ask the tough questions: Do I want to
give for strategic reasons—or is my desire simply an emotional
response to a particularly poignant appeal? Is the need truly
justified? Can this organization (or person) produce the results
they're promising?

Imagine getting a call from a stockbroker who wanted you
to invest in a particular company. No matter how good the
pitch sounded, you would probably ask to see additional information, such as the company's prospectus. And if you purchased the stock, chances are good that you'd check the
progress of your investment on the financial pages at least
monthly—if not daily.

By contrast, most of us give by writing a check and then
putting the matter out of our minds. We don't think much
about giving in the first place, and we spend even less time
monitoring the progress of our "investment." But like financial investing, strategic giving demands we do "due diligence."
Before we give, we have to do our homework.

My good friend, Pat MacMillan, is a managment consul-
tant and the author of *Hiring Excellence*. He has spent more

time and energy studying strategic and leveraged giving than anyone I know. I've appropriated some of his best thoughts for inclusion here. According to Pat's analysis, strategic, effective ministries exhibit certain definable characteristics. As you evaluate giving opportunities to your church, the missionaries you know, any parachurch groups, Christian organizations, or other charities, evaluate the ministry based on the following questions.

1. Are the leaders marked by godly characteristics? Christian leaders—pastors, missionaries, organization heads, and so forth—should be men and women of character, integrity, and vision. They must be competent and qualified to do their jobs, and they should have a biblically based vision that can be communicated to their donors in clear, measurable terms. Most important, they should have a growing, vibrant relationship with Jesus Christ. If you cannot trust a group's leaders, you should not be giving money to that organization.

2. Is the ministry active in God's "hot spots"? Some well-meaning churches, missionaries, campus workers, and other ministry-oriented Christians develop plans and programs assuming God will bless their good intentions. Others, however, take the time to find out what God is doing and where he is working and align themselves with his purposes.

Peter Wagner, a well-known missiologist and author, points to patterns in world events as evidence of the Holy Spirit's work. When the Iron Curtain fell, for example, Christians saw God move in amazing ways through Communism's former strongholds. Today, China and Latin America are among the world's evangelistic "hot spots." Whether the action is happening in a church across the street or on a mission field a half a world away, strategic ministries are working in God's "hot spots."

3. Is the ministry innovative? Strategic ministries often create, experiment, and challenge. Instead of getting bogged down in a routine, they try new methods and ideas—without letting go of their principles or their message. They see things other ministries might not, such as how to turn a short-term opportunity into a vehicle for long-term growth.

They also make mistakes. If you want your church or organization to be innovative, you need to be willing to tolerate errors. Effective ministries take risks—and when they make mistakes, they don't cover them up. Instead, they use them as a platform for discovery.

4. Is the ministry growing and cooperative? Strategic ministries achieve results. This progress, coupled with the clear vision and sense of purpose communicated by the leaders, motivates donors to invest in and be part of the ministry. Ministry workers are likewise attracted and motivated—which ultimately leads to even greater ministry growth.

In the same vein, strategic ministries are willing to partner with like-minded people and organizations. When the Billy Graham team comes to a city, for example, they don't build an organization to launch their crusades. Instead, they work with existing churches and ministries, pooling the resources of countless committed Christians—and as a result, denominational barriers crumble.

5. Is the ministry goal-oriented? Strategic ministries have a clear sense of what God wants them to do and how he wants them to do it. Effective churches, missionaries, and parachurch groups are committed to their goals—regardless of how their actions might be perceived by their members or supporters. While they are open to suggestions, strategic ministries never let funding—or a lack of it—dictate their goals and decisions.

6. *Is the ministry accountable?* Having established goals, strategic ministries hold themselves and their staff accountable to accomplish these objectives. Instead of measuring the organization's activity level, effective ministries measure progress and results. One well-known family ministry commissioned an outside researcher to measure how their organization was affecting families. Such an independent analysis can stack results against goals to provide an accurate evaluation of ministry effectiveness.

As you evaluate a church or ministry, ask yourself questions: *Are the elders or deacons strong enough to hold the leaders accountable? Is there a credible board of directors in place?* If you support an individual missionary, *who are the people he or she has to report to?*

Financially, too, you should check for accountability structures. Strategic ministries have checks and balances in place to ensure that their operations are above reproach.

7. *Is the ministry endorsed by a strong track record?* The best indicator of what a ministry will do is what it has done. Eloquent appeals and effective fund-raising do not always signal effectiveness in ministry. Instead of analyzing an organization's "look" or style of communication, focus on the ministry and the results it has achieved.

Strategic giving is, to some degree, dependent on where God has placed you and who he has brought into your life, from a relationship standpoint. If your teenager becomes active in a youth group or a high school ministry, God may lead you to give to that organization. If your church plants a mission church overseas, you might consider becoming part of that effort, financially. You will never be able to give to every strategic and effective church, ministry, or missionary. Instead of spreading yourself thin in an attempt to be part of every good work, consider where God has placed you, and why.

As you evaluate the churches, ministries, and people you support, if you detect a weakness in leadership, accountability structure, ministry track record, or any other critical area, you will not be doing God's kingdom any favors by maintaining your support. Sometimes ineffective ministries need a financial wake-up call to spur them on. Sometimes, too, a once-vital ministry that has fulfilled its original mission may need to shut down or reorient its focus. Your prayerful decision to discontinue support—coupled with a letter or telephone call of gentle explanation—may be the most strategic way you can use your resources.

Instead of spreading yourself thin in an attempt to be part of every good work, consider where God has placed you, and why.

Even if an organization or individual is doing a good job meeting a legitimate need, God may want you to pull back, financially, so that others can take your place. Every dollar you give is a dollar that someone else could be giving. Perhaps God wants someone else to step up to the plate and take advantage of the giving opportunity your vacancy would create.

Finally, do not assume that your commitment to give to a particular ministry must be a long-term obligation. Instead, take time each year to evaluate your giving. Keep a list of the people and organizations you support, and pray about whether or not you should continue.

LEVERAGED GIVING

NOT ONLY DO RESULTS SIGNAL AN effective ministry, they are also a key indicator of efficiency. Efficient ministries are "leveraged": They get results, maximizing their own impact and providing the greatest returns on a donor's financial investment.

One of the best contemporary examples of leveraged giving I can think of is the *Jesus* film, which chronicles the life and message of Christ. The film has been translated into four hundred languages and seen by well over a billion people—more than twenty percent of the world's population! Based on how the film is currently being used for evangelism, I know that for every dollar given to that effort, ten people will hear the Gospel.

In the same way, when you give to support a seminary student or a missionary, your giving may go far beyond that initial investment. One trained pastor can impact hundreds, and even thousands, of people in a lifetime of ministry. That's how leveraged giving works on a practical, powerful level.

"Matching" programs, too, can significantly leverage your giving. If your employer offers to match your charitable contributions, take advantage of the opportunity. Likewise, if an individual donor who supports your church or ministry offers to match all contributions made toward a particular project (such as a building fund or the missions budget), recognize the offer for what it is: a timely opportunity to maximize the efficiency of your giving.

A scriptural parallel to leveraged giving may be seen in the parable of the talents, recounted in Matthew 25. Before embarking on a journey, a man summoned his servants and asked them to handle his money. The first servant got five talents (more than $5,000). The next one received two talents ($2,000), while the third man was given just one talent ($1,000).

The master was gone for a long time. When he returned, he found that the fellow who had received five talents had invested the money and doubled his holdings. Likewise, the

one with two talents had put the money to work and earned
two more. But the man who had been given only one talent
had nothing to show for himself. Instead of investing the
money, he had nervously buried it in the ground, digging it up
only when the master returned.

Branding the fellow lazy, wicked, and worthless, the master ordered the fearful servant tossed out into the darkness.
But for the others—the men who had doubled his money—
the master had nothing but praise. "Well done, good and
faithful servant!" he said to both of them. "You have been
faithful with a few things; I will put you in charge of many
things. Come and share your master's happiness!"

Like the fearful servant, some churches and ministry
workers plod along, unwilling to get in on God's action for
fear of where he might lead. They drain their cash resources,
with little or nothing to show for it in the end. Leveraged
ministries, on the other hand, put the contributions of their
members or supporters to work in a way that enhances their
overall effectiveness. Like the wise servants, they pursue the
highest return, generating the maximum result for every dollar they receive.

When your giving is strategic and leveraged, you—like the
wise money managers—will be worthy of the Lord's approval:
"Well done, good and faithful servant!"

GETTING STARTED

JUST AS WISE INVESTING CALLS FOR careful research and
regular monitoring, so strategic giving demands your attention and time. While not everyone gets drawn into a scam like
the one Steve faced, almost all of us have made strategic giving errors at one time or another. Secular philanthropic advis-

ers, for example, often tell their clients to give according to their "passions" or "interests." But, as the parable of the talents reminds us, the goal of any steward is to please his master. Consequently, God's priorities define how we should give. Our personal interests and desires—no matter how "right" or "noble" they seem to us—must be abandoned if they are not in sync with God's giving priorities.

Our personal interests and desires—no matter how "right" or "noble" they seem to us—must be abandoned if they are not in sync with God's giving priorities.

As you begin to give strategically, keep a file of the requests you receive. Contrast the various ministries, individuals, or organizations, and mark any that you would like to contribute to, even if you cannot send a donation today.

Take "vision trips"—as I recommended in chapter 6—to gain a sense of urgency and excitement about what God is doing in the world around you. If traveling is physically or financially impossible, get your information vicariously by hosting a missionary in your home or meeting with others who are actively involved in ministry.

Develop an "expert" list. Maintain contacts with people who understand the principles of strategic and leveraged giving, and who can interpret world events to help you pinpoint "hot spots" or identify ministries or organizations with strong track records.

Finally, watch out for the "yellow flags" God often sends to warn us away from foolish decisions. If you and your spouse cannot agree about a gift that one of you wants to make, take it as God's signal to hold off. If a ministry suddenly loses a key funding source, or if you discover that the bulk of the organization's revenues come from one single donor, do a little digging into the ministry's overall health and effectiveness. Likewise, if you detect a weakening in a church or ministry's momentum or a sudden change in its leadership or organizational structure, look extra closely before you make any financial commitments.

As you exercise discernment, beware of ministry claims that sound too good to be true. In 1995, many wealthy people and charitable organizations gave millions of dollars to the Foundation for New Era Philanthropy, which promised to double the funds in six months with matching gifts from anonymous philanthropists. The mystery philanthropists turned out to be non-existent, and when New Era filed for bankruptcy, people who had expected to see their giving or their resources double were sorely disappointed.

If you gave to a ministry that was involved with New Era, or if you have ever been taken in by a scam as Steve was, remember that God is bigger than your mistakes. Cliff Barrows, music and program director for the Billy Graham team, tells the story of a young Indian weaver who worked at his loom. The weaver studied a pattern, adding row after row of colorful threads to the design. One day a tourist stopped to watch the man work.

"What happens if you make a mistake?" the tourist asked.

"Oh," the weaver smiled. "If I make a mistake, I go tell the teacher. He comes over and makes a mark on the pattern, working my mistake into the larger design. Then I keep weaving. When I am finished, I cannot find the mistake, no matter how hard I look. It has become part of the pattern."

That's how God works. When news of the New Era scandal broke, it made headlines across the country and sent a jolt throughout the Christian community. Even so, God's work continued without a hitch. (In a remarkable testimony, ministries that lost money in the scandal found their funds replaced when other Christian organizations—those who had profited from New Era before the scam collapsed—returned the money they had received.)

The Lord wants us to give with wisdom, of course, but our giving—no matter how much we give—is only a small part of his bigger pattern. If your giving has not been as strategic or effective as it could have been, use your mistakes and the principles outlined in this chapter to change your direction. Be like Steve. He refused to quit—and today his giving is strategic, generous, and more powerful than he could have ever imagined.

For most people, the question of how much to give their children is not really a question at all; they just expect to leave everything they have to their kids. But there's a lot more to effective estate planning than simply figuring out how to get your money into the hands of your heirs. And before you think about passing on wealth, be sure you are leaving your children a legacy of wisdom, as well.

Giving to Your Children
Passing Down More than Money

YOU WORK HARD TO EARN A LIVING AND PROVIDE for your family. You buy things such as houses, cars, and furniture, and you try your best to sock away enough cash to pay for college or retirement. Accumulating money and possessions is a normal part of everday life. But have you ever stopped to think—really *think*—about where all your wealth will ultimately wind up?

Just as you can give money to charity wisely or unwisely, you have strategic decisions to make when you think about passing on wealth to your kids.

Strategic giving to charity, as described in the last chapter, is one way to allocate your resources, either through current giving or via your estate plan. Your other option—which is frankly the *only* choice most people consider when they think about what will happen to their money—is to give it to your heirs: your children, your extended family members, and your friends. And just as you can give money to charity wisely or unwisely, you have strategic decisions to make when you think about passing on wealth to your kids. While this chapter focuses primarily on giving to your children, the principles we'll cover can also be applied to the broader circle of your family and friends.

Scripture tells the story of a young man who asked his father to give him his share of the family estate (see Luke 15:11–31). When the father consented, dividing his property between his two sons, the young fellow took his money and hit the road. He put as much distance as possible between himself and his father's influence, and then he began living it up, squandering his inheritance on parties and wild living. It wasn't long before the money ran out, and—to make matters worse—a severe famine hit the country where the young fellow had settled.

Financial assets should not be passed on without first handing down a healthy portion of wisdom.

Finding himself in a desperate financial situation, the man got a job feeding pigs. He was so hungry that he would've eaten the pigs' slop, had anyone offered it to him—but no one did.

Finally it hit him: He was starving to death, far from home, while his father's hired hands had food to spare. Right then and there he decided to go home and ask his father for two things: forgiveness and a job.

But the son was in for a big surprise. His father saw him coming, and, filled with compassion, he ran to greet his son. Catching his son in a giant bear hug, the father hardly seemed to hear the boy as he confessed his sin and his unworthiness. Instead the exuberant father ordered up a huge celebration.

His son—the child he feared he might never see again—had come home.

While Luke uses this story to illustrate our heavenly Father's love for us, it also serves as a poignant example of the twin aspects of an inheritance. When they hear the term "inheritance," most people think only about passing on material *wealth*. In reality, though, *wisdom* is a legacy of even greater value. As Ecclesiastes 7:11–12 puts it,

> Wisdom, like an inheritance, is a good thing
>   and benefits those who see the sun.
> Wisdom is a shelter as money is a shelter,
>   but the advantage of knowledge is this:
>   that wisdom preserves the life of its possessor.

As you think about giving to your children, remember that financial assets should not be passed on without first handing down a healthy portion of wisdom. To help you transfer wealth to your children as strategically as possible, this chapter is divided into two parts. First, you build a legacy of wisdom by teaching your children how to handle money. Once that foundation is in place, you can then concentrate on the issues that define effective estate planning: How much to give, when to give, and what "form" your gifts should take.

TEACHING YOUR CHILDREN TO HANDLE MONEY

AMANDA? AMANDA . . . WHERE ARE YOU?" The woman's voice was marked by impatience and fatigue. Her daughter had been beside her just a minute ago. "Amanda, come here!"

"Here I am!" replied the child as she rounded a corner in the toy store and joined her mother and the baby in the checkout line. "Look what I found. Can we get it?"

How well your children ultimately learn financial lessons is dependent, to a large degree, on how well you manage your own resources.

Amanda's mother peered down at the brightly colored box in her daughter's hands. It held a small doll whose main feature seemed to be a cascade of shimmering hair trimmed with what looked like ten or twelve ribbons, clips, and bows.

"No. Put it back."

"Please, Mom," Amanda begged, "I really want it. I *love* it."

"Amanda," her mother said, "you have a plenty of dolls—and you hardly even play with them! Besides, we came here to buy diapers and a birthday present for your sister. We don't have money for a doll today—money doesn't grow on trees, you know."

"Please—"

Just then the baby started to cry. As the cashier rang up the diapers, Amanda's mother fumbled in her purse for a pacifier and her wallet.

"Please, Mom. I—"

"Oh, all right!" Amanda's mother grabbed the doll and tossed it onto the counter. "But don't ask me for anything else today!"

Amanda beamed, throwing her arms around her mother's legs. "Thanks, Mom. You're the best!"

This illustration—which reflects countless similar stories we experience or witness all the time—reveals both the challenges and opportunities we face when it comes to teaching our children to handle money wisely. Financial instruction can begin even before the first dime gets dropped into the piggy bank. How well your children ultimately learn the lessons is dependent, to a large degree, on how well you manage your own resources. As Judy and I often remind each other, "More is caught than taught."

You can use all sorts of methods to teach your children how to earn, save, invest, and spend wisely—methods that Judy and I used with our own children and then outlined in our book, *Raising Money-Smart Kids*. But no matter which techniques you choose, the bottom line in teaching wisdom to children is that children learn responsibility by having responsibility.

Instead of limiting your children's experiences in managing money or "covering" for them when they mishandle an allowance, encourage them to take responsibility for their own decisions. As you teach and train them, keep three basic principles in mind: If you want to give your children a legacy of wisdom, they must understand the concept of *limited resources*, they have to recognize the benefits of *delayed gratification*, and they need to develop a *strong work ethic*.

Limited Resources

When Amanda's mother gave in and bought her the doll, she sent a mixed financial message. She *said* that she didn't have money for a doll and that money does not grow on trees. But what she *did* told another story: that the supply of money was unlimited and that by asking or begging hard enough Amanda could get anything she wanted.

In reality, of course, you cannot have everything. There will always be unlimited ways to spend money. To make wise choices between these alternatives, kids need to understand the concept of *limited resources*.

The best way to teach this principle is to give your child the experience of living with a limited amount of money. For younger children, a weekly allowance—along with an explanation of the types of purchases it would need to cover—can provide invaluable "hands-on" training. Few exercises are harder on a parent than watching his or her child make unwise spending decisions and then have to live with the consequences. But until a child learns to prioritize his or her needs and wants, recognizing that the dollar won't buy both candy *and* stickers (or, for older children, stereo equipment *and* clothing), the child won't be able to make the hard choices that life is sure to send his or her way.

Amanda's mother may have missed an opportunity to teach her daughter about limited resources, but she—unfortunately—gave Amanda another powerful lesson. In her successful quest for the doll, Amanda enjoyed a first-rate opportunity to hone her manipulation skills and techniques. Begging, whining, flattering, throwing temper tantrums, even taking advantage of a parent's preoccupation with a crying baby or some other detail are all skills that children learn and parents (often unwittingly) reinforce. Instead of teaching her daughter how to accept the constraints of limited resources, Amanda's mother taught her how to get her way.

Delayed Gratification

Delayed gratification is the willingness and ability to sacrifice immediate desires in order to achieve a future benefit. This concept—which runs contrary to a child's nature and to almost everything the world teaches about immediate gratification—can spell the difference between long-term financial success and failure.

When our children were growing up, we required each of them to have a savings account. They were responsible for contributing to the account, and they used their allowances,

**Delayed gratification is the willingness and ability
to sacrifice immediate desires in order to achieve
a future benefit.**

money they earned from doing special chores, and cash they
received for birthdays or Christmas gifts to build their balances. Then, when they wanted to buy something like a new
tennis racquet, a stereo, or a special party dress, they could dip
into their savings. In addition to giving our kids the thrill of
being able to acquire something they really wanted by
saving—and waiting—for it, this system reinforced the concept of limited resources. When funds are depleted, you cannot buy something you might like to have—no matter how
badly you want or need it.

A Strong Work Ethic

Learning how to handle limited resources and to postpone
gratification are just two of the marks of financial wisdom and
maturity. The third principle that must be taught and culti-
vated in our children is a strong work ethic.

Amanda's mother may have meant well, but when she gave
in and bought the doll, she missed a golden opportunity to
teach her daughter a basic lesson about financial management:
namely, that you can never get something for nothing. Everything costs, and there is always a trade-off between work and
rewards.

Instead of simply buying the doll outright, Amanda's
mother could have offered her daughter the opportunity to
work and earn money—which she could then use to purchase
the doll on her own. Such independent purchasing power is a

tangible benefit of labor. Experiences such as this reinforce the relationship between time and money, or effort and reward, and can motivate a child to develop a strong and lasting work ethic.

In addition to helping children understand the link between work and economic rewards, the opportunity to work—with or without pay—offers at least two other significant benefits. First, it demonstrates obedience to God's command that we work (see Eph. 4:28). Additionally, working hard to get a job done can fill a child with a vital sense of satisfaction and accomplishment (which, in turn, reinforces the strong work ethic).

The importance of teaching financial wisdom to your children cannot be underestimated. Imagine, for example, what would happen if Amanda were to reach adulthood without ever learning or understanding the concepts of limited resources, delayed gratification, and a strong work ethic. Failing to recognize any limits on the money supply, she would look to her husband to provide unlimited financing for her desires. If he refused her demands or was unable to meet them, she might turn to her parents, cementing her dependency on their generosity and driving a wedge into her marriage relationship. Without an understanding of delayed gratification, Amanda would rely on the manipulation skills she learned as a child to get her own way. And with no solid work ethic of her own, she could easily become intolerant of her husband's need and desire to earn a living, sabotaging his work ethic and, ultimately, their marriage.

Obviously, women are not the only ones who need financial wisdom. An adult man who has never learned to earn and manage money wisely may lead his family into real financial difficulty. Think back to the story of the wayward son. With no appreciation for the value or necessity of hard work, and no apparent grasp of his limited resources, he was doomed. He wanted everything immediately—from his inheritance to the lifestyle it initially provided. How much pain would he (and his father) have been spared had he only learned the concepts of limited resources, delayed gratification, and hard work!

But there's another lesson in this story. When the son came back, repentant and humble, the father could have said something like, "Ha! I knew something like this would happen. Now you've gone and lost all your money—and you can bet I'm not giving you any more! If you want to stick around here, you're going to have to start earning your keep. Go on and feed the pigs—go on and get out of my sight!"

Plenty of fathers would have responded this way—and with understandable cause. But God, our heavenly Father, does not. Instead, he gives us gifts we don't earn or deserve. This is what generosity and grace are all about.

As parents, we want our children to understand that God is a gracious God, and he may choose to give us gifts for no reason whatsoever.

As important (and time-consuming) as it is to teach your children how to handle limited resources, delay gratification, and work to earn rewards, you can still feel free to give them money and gifts from time to time. All the economic resources that we ultimately end up with are gifts from God. As parents, we want our children to understand that God is a gracious God, and he may choose to give us gifts for no reason whatsoever.

How Much Money Should You Give Your Children?

As critical as it is to teach your children to handle money wisely, it is just as important to exercise discretion and insight yourself when you think about giving wealth to your children, both currently and through your estate. The Bible does not give specific guidelines as to how much inheritance we should leave our children or when we should give it to them, but by using the broader principles outlined in Scripture, we can get a good handle on the answers to these questions.

The first issue to address is whether or not you ought to give money to your children. For most people, the question of how much to give is not really a question at all; they just expect to leave all of their assets to their children. But there's a lot more to effective estate planning than simply figuring out how to get your money into the hands of your heirs.

In general, four basic questions can help you define your position:

- Is giving money to your children good stewardship?
- Do they have the wisdom to handle an inheritance?
- Though not wrong, is leaving an inheritance for your children wise?
- Do your children or grandchildren have any special needs that God might want you to provide for?

Is Giving Money to Your Children Good Stewardship?

Dr. James Dobson often speaks about giving money to children. Noting that he has rarely seen any good come out of leaving wealth to children, Jim always tells people not to leave their kids an amount that would ensure or guarantee their financial independence. Instead of stockpiling wealth for future generations, Jim believes that people who have the ability to give away significant sums of money would be wise to consider using their resources for kingdom purposes.

For many people, advice like that is a hard pill to swallow. Watching faces in the audience as Dobson speaks, I can almost read people's minds. Some wrestle with a desire to see the business they have built or the wealth they have amassed passed on to their descendents as a testimony to their own success and accomplishments. Others fear the potentially negative ramifications that can occur when children discover they have been "disinherited." Still others sit there, mouths agape, wondering how to process this information that runs so counter to everything they have ever been taught to do or expect.

I respect Dr. Dobson's advice, and I am equally opposed to hoarding wealth when generosity would be a better option. But I think Jim would agree with me when I say that the concept of good stewardship involves more than just giving all or indiscriminately to God's kingdom. To be an effective steward of the money God gives you, you need to begin by asking, "What would God want me to do with these resources?"

I was once approached by a couple who had three children, including a son who was involved in an immoral, irresponsible lifestyle. In the interest of what they thought was "good stewardship," they had all but decided to leave the wayward child out of their wills. Giving him money, they reasoned, would be tantamount to wasting God's resources.

The only problem was that they did not feel comfortable about the decision. They had prayed about it and sought the advice of several wise and mature Christians, yet they still struggled emotionally with the idea of disinheriting their son. They asked me what I thought they should do.

I immediately breathed a quick prayer: "Lord, help!" Then, prompted by the Holy Spirit, I asked the couple a pointed question. "Would your son be more likely to repent and come to Christ if he were disinherited, and understood why, or if you were to include him in your wills?"

The couple replied without hesitation. "He'd be more likely to come to Christ if he was in our will. But our assets belong to God—we can't just use them to benefit our son, can we?"

Instead of answering that question, I asked another one: "Do you think God would spend the amount that you would leave your son in order to encourage him to become a Christian?"

I could see the light dawn in their eyes. "Yes," they said, "he would." And with that, it became an easy decision. They would include their son in their wills.

In this case, asking the "right" questions made all the difference in the couple's financial decision. Sometimes, though, you can be too close to an issue, emotionally speaking, to think clearly and ask the right questions. When that happens, it is important to pray diligently for God's direction and to seek professional counsel from a Christian perspective.

Do Your Children Have the Wisdom to Handle an Inheritance?

Deciding whether or not to leave money to your children, or how much to give them, often raises more questions than it answers. If your kids are young, you may not know how they will handle money, or even if they will want to manage it in a godly fashion.

If your children are older, consider these issues: How would a large—or small—inheritance impact their marriages? Have they demonstrated wise stewardship in other financial matters? Would they be apt to squander an inheritance—or would they invest it in God's kingdom by giving to meet the physical and spiritual needs of others? And what if one child is more (or less) able to manage an inheritance than the others? Do you distribute your assets equally to avoid sibling conflict, or do you give more to the one who can handle it?

If you want to include your children in your will but are unsure about their ability to handle money, consider giving them a token inheritance now.

In addition to praying for guidance on questions like these, you can obtain some concrete answers by conducting financial experiments with your children. If you want to include them in your will but are unsure about their ability to handle money, consider giving them a token inheritance now. Not only will this exercise give you a window on your children's financial habits, abilities, and priorities, but by "practicing" with a small amount of money, your children can learn from their mistakes and benefit from your guidance. And as a matter of fact, by giving your children larger sums of money as they get older (and wiser), you can reap significant tax benefits—a subject I'll cover in greater detail later in this chapter.

Questions such as how much to leave your children or whether or not to distribute your estate equally take a backseat to the overriding issue, which is whether or not you have given your children a legacy of wisdom. If you have not passed on wisdom, don't pass on wealth. To do otherwise can be extraordinarily detrimental to the child.

Remember Amanda? If her parents gave her a large inheritance without ever giving her the discipline, wisdom, and responsibility to handle money, they could easily be launching a torpedo into her life, as well as her marriage. You would not give alcohol to an alcoholic; likewise, you need to think twice before giving money to someone who is ill-equipped to handle it.

Giving Money May Not Be Wrong—But Is It Wise?

Over the years, I've been privileged to speak to various groups of donors on behalf of the ministries that they support. I always enjoy these seminars, as most of the people in the audience are genuinely interested in learning more about biblical principles of handling money. Many of the donors are business owners or other professionals, so the issue of passing on wealth is of prime importance to them, and they are always very attentive.

They are not, however, always very accepting of my advice. I tell them the same thing I am telling you: It's not biblically *wrong* to pass on wealth to your children, but it may not always be *wise*. Most people's estates are typically worth a lot more than they would ever guess. When you add up the value of your your home, insurance policies, company pension plans, investments, savings accounts, cars, jewelry, and other personal assets or property, chances are that the combined total could be invested to generate enough earnings so that your children would not have to work to provide for themselves or their spouses in the future. If so, then you run the risk of short-circuiting the wisdom process we covered in the first part of this chapter. By removing the need to earn a living, you might also destroy the motivation to work—and your kids might only learn the concept of "limited resources" as they watch their nest egg disappear.

Do Your Children or Grandchildren Have Any Special Needs?

Leaving too much money to your children can be dangerous to their future. But before you opt to leave them out of your will and give everything you have to charity, I want to raise one final question: What if one of your children (or grandchildren) has a special need?

The cost of caring for a physically or mentally handicapped child can be beyond comprehension. While the Bible does charge us with the responsibility of providing for our family, Scripture does not mandate exactly how this charge plays out, practically speaking. I believe that parents have a responsibility to provide for their children, handicapped or not. As a grandparent, I would also be willing to share the financial burden, particularly if God had given me the resources to do so.

I have five children. At this point, only two of them have children of their own. I do not know what the future holds for my family, financially or health-wise. Therefore, Judy and I have decided to make some provision for the unknown, leaving a portion of our estate to our children, more as a precautionary measure than anything else.

If, like us, you have decided to give an inheritance to your children, deciding how much to give them is a function of some of the very same questions we have already covered. In addition to evaluating their financial wisdom and abilities, ask yourself what needs they have that God might want you to help meet. Do they need help buying their first home, educating their children, or starting a business? As you decide how much money to give your children, you should prayerfully consider the level of financial involvement God would want you to assume in their lives.

Hand-in-hand with the "how much" question is the "when" question. You can give an inheritance to your children through your estate, of course, but it might make more sense to begin giving money to them now, before you die.

WHEN SHOULD YOU GIVE MONEY TO YOUR CHILDREN?

WHEN EACH OF THEIR FOUR CHILDREN reached his or her eighteenth birthday, Sam and Becky gave them a portion of their inheritance. Their goal was to find out how the kids would handle a small amount of money—and, consequently, how they'd be apt to handle more.

Sam and Becky's children may have had good intentions, but being young and relatively inexperienced in financial management, they pretty much wasted the money. But, like the Bible's wayward son who returned to his father, the children learned some valuable lessons from their mistakes. Today, Sam and Becky periodically give their children lump sums of money, tax-free, and they do a masterful job of handling it wisely.

By demonstrating generosity toward their children, Sam and Becky are sowing and reaping the benefits of "lifetime giving." In addition to giving their kids "hands on" experience and training in financial managment, Sam and Becky's gifts have provided blessings that reach beyond material values. Family vacations that otherwise would not have been possible have become an affordable reality, thanks to Sam and Becky's generosity. Likewise, their gifts have opened the door for a number of their grandchildren to attend private Christian schools—an education that Sam and Becky see as a valuable and practical investment in their family's future.

Many of our clients have adopted a similar outlook on giving to their children. One couple offered to pay the life insurance premiums for their son-in-law until he could afford to make the payments out of his own salary. Another man gave his children money toward the down payment on their first home. While practical helps like these obviously involve a financial cost, the non-material benefits they provide can make a significant difference in your children's lives and their ability to raise a family.

Another advantage of lifetime giving, as I mentioned earlier, is the effect it can have on your taxes. Under the current tax law, you can give away $10,000 per year to as many individuals as you like. In other words, a husband and wife together could give $20,000 a year to each of their four children—thereby reducing the size (and taxability) of their estate by $80,000 each year. By including sons- and daughters-in-law and grandchildren in the distribution plan, the size (and taxability) of the estate could shrink even further. When you are looking for creative ways to minimize estate taxes, taking advantage of the annual gift exclusion can make good economic sense.

One of the best things about giving money to your children (or grandchildren) is the opportunity you get to watch them use it to enrich their lives. Unfortunately, lifetime giving also means you have to watch them make mistakes.

One of the best things about giving money to your children (or grandchildren) is the opportunity you get to watch them use it to enrich their lives—an opportunity you would otherwise forego if you waited to distribute your assets through your estate. Perhaps one of your children feels called to be a missionary. Would a financial gift from you help him or her make the vision a reality? Likewise, your generosity toward your children, exercised with wisdom, can open doors and alleviate financial burdens when it comes to things like starting a business, buying a first home, or funding your grandchildren's college education.

Unfortunately, lifetime giving also means you have to watch them make mistakes. While you need to be ready to offer financial guidance and advice when your kids ask for it, you must also remember that a gift is a gift. Once you give money to your children, it is theirs to spend, save, or give away as they will. You cannot give money with strings attached.

For some parents and grandparents, this poses an almost impossible challenge. Instead of giving money freely, we may be tempted to want something in return: phone calls, visits during the holidays, a license to "meddle" in our children's marriages, and so on. But those kinds of expectations run contrary to the spirit of generous living. When you make a gift to your children, be sure it is exactly that: a gift.

Despite the benefits associated with lifetime giving, you may feel financially unable or emotionally unwilling (for whatever reason) to begin passing on your wealth right now. In that case, providing for your heirs via a strategic estate plan becomes all the more important. In the next chapter, we'll address some of the critical issues you need to consider as you draft or revise your will.

WHAT SHOULD YOU GIVE YOUR CHILDREN?

ONCE YOU DECIDE HOW MUCH TO leave your children and when to give it to them, you need to consider the form in which your assets will be left. Should you leave the farm? What about the family business? Is it better to leave cash, stocks, or real estate?

In general, the answer to the "form" question is simple: Assets should be left in a form that will allow your children to accomplish their God-given goals and build their skills and strengths. Typically, this means that gifts should be left in cash or other liquid assets, such as stocks and bonds, which can be sold easily and quickly.

While challenges are associated with giving almost any portion of your estate to your children, perhaps the most difficult asset to transfer is a closely held family business. More than 95 percent of all the businesses in the United States are privately held, family-owned enterprises. Almost always the temptation is to keep the business "in the family," transferring it to one or more of your adult children without regard for their abilities, interests, or inheritance needs.

Richard spent years trying to figure out how to get the business he built into the hands of his six children. Each of the kids had different interests and talents, and their ages spanned a fifteen-year gamut. Finally, desperate for a workable solution, Richard asked me what he should do.

"Sell the company," I advised.

Richard was flabbergasted. "I created that company!" he protested. "It's mine—I worked hard to make it what it is today. I can't just sell it like some old car or a piece of furniture!"

I reminded Richard of the fundamental truth: God owns it all. Richard may have worked hard to make his business grow, but, ultimately, it belonged to God. Until he took his own ego out of the equation and began looking at his business as *God's* asset, he would never be able to handle it properly.

If you have a business, a farm, or some other large nonliquid asset, consider converting it into cash before you pass it on to your heirs. An Atlanta family who is strapped for cash and squeezed into a two-bedroom home might welcome a cash inheritance much more happily than they would receive the family potato farm in Idaho. Likewise, a son who is given money that he can invest in his successful landscaping business would benefit more from a cash gift than he would if he were handed a bakery that he had no interest in or ability to manage.

By converting a business to cash, you also remove the issue of sibling conflict from the equation. Unless one of your children has the talents, skills, or business experience to clearly mark him or her as the "heir apparent," the question of who will actually run the company can be divisive. And even when the choice is obvious, underlying tensions and resentment can still crop up if children feel they have been overlooked or treated unfairly.

As you consider the form your assets are in, remember that they belong to God. Instead of thinking about how you want them to be allocated or managed, ask yourself how he would want you to distribute them. Think about your heirs and their individual needs. Then, take steps to convert your assets into a form that can be effectively and efficiently used.

DYNAMIC DECISIONS: REVIEW YOUR PLAN

ESTATE PLANNING — THE HOWS, WHENS, AND WHATS of giving to charity and your heirs—is a dynamic process. Just as you must periodically reevaluate your charitable giving strategies, so you need to review your plan for giving money to your children. The issues and decisions you face today will change as your children grow and mature.

> **Just as you must periodically reevaluate your charitable giving strategies, so you need to review your plan for giving money to your children.**

As you ask yourself questions and think through your answers, remember that so much of what is strategic or effective in estate planning depends on your individual children. One of our clients feels perfectly comfortable leaving significant sums of money to his offspring. Another client plans to give everything to charity. Both clients are godly, mature Christians. Their individual families, though, are vastly different.

In the coming chapter you'll find out how to put your plans into practice by designing a sound and strategic will. Your will is the written testimony to all the decisions and choices you have made in this chapter. While these decisions (and others) will provide you with a strategic approach to estate planning, you should meet with a financial professional to discuss the specific tools and techniques appropriate to your family's individual needs. As you choose a financial advisor, be sure to select someone who can provide a knowledgeable, biblical perspective on issues like the ones we have covered here.

Once you have the documents in place to meet your family's needs, get in the habit of reviewing your wills regularly—at least every few years. As your legacy of wisdom grows stronger in your children, you may feel the freedom to pass on more wealth as well, both during your lifetime—when the opportunity for training is the greatest—and through your estate.

Almost everyone agrees that a will is an important document—but only about twenty percent of us actually take the time to make one. Drafting a will may sound intimidating, but it's really nothing more than a series of six critical decisions. With the help of a qualified financial advisor, you can avoid "will paralysis" and provide effectively for your children and for charity.

eleven

Giving Through Your Will

Six Critical Decisions You Need to Make

HAVE YOU EVER DRAWN A ROAD MAP TO HELP someone find his way to your house? Atlanta is such a big city, with new construction and roads being built almost everywhere you look, that it's often easier to send a map to someone than it is to give a complex series of verbal directions. With a well-drawn map, your guest can have no question about which direction to go or which turn to take. A good map provides clarity.

Your will is the financial map your friends and relatives can use to distribute your estate assets according to your desires.

Your will is the financial map your friends and relatives can use to distribute your estate assets according to your desires. Even if you have enjoyed a lifetime of generous giving, chances are that your property, insurance policies, and other assets will add up to a significant sum. The better the map you leave for your heirs, the more effectively they will be able to follow the course you have charted when it comes time to divide up your estate.

Most people readily acknowledge the value of having a will. Even so, it's estimated that as many as 80 percent of us don't have one. And according to one survey, more than two-thirds of America's practicing lawyers do not even have current estate documents!

The decisions you have made so far—including lifestyle choices, charitable giving patterns, and generosity toward your children—all play a major role in determining the amount of assets you will have to pass on through your estate. At this point, you may be tempted to skim this chapter, thinking you will concentrate on drafting a will at some point in the future, when you have "more time." Let me encourage you to take time now, while the issues and decisions you have made are still fresh in your mind, to meet with an attorney or a professional financial advisor. If you wait, you may find yourself caught in the phenomenon I call "will paralysis."

OVERCOMING "WILL PARALYSIS"

THE INITIAL DRAFTING OF A WILL is *important*, but it is rarely *urgent*. Most of us would sooner spend the time and money paying our bills than we would making a will. In the grand scheme of things, a will is more important than your electric bill, but if the power company cuts off your electricity, it won't take you long to identify the past-due bill as your more urgent problem.

Unfortunately, most of us only act on the "urgent" things in life, waiting until the "important" things become immediate problems before we attend to them. You can live forever without a will—but if you die without one, your family will have an urgent, immediate problem.

You can live forever without a will—but if you die without one, your family will have an urgent, immediate problem.

When I said that as many as 80 percent of Americans do not have a will, that is not entirely correct. If you do not have a will, the state you live in will provide one for you—and you can bet you'll owe a hefty sum in taxes, administrative fees, and other expenses. Not only that, but with a state-supplied will, you run the very serious risk that your assets (including your minor children!) will wind up going to someone you would not have chosen to receive them.

Why would anyone *not* take the time to draft a will? Apart from an unwillingness to accept our own mortality, the single greatest contributor to will paralysis is the fact that we do not understand *how* to make a will. Most people who have wills only draft or revise them a few times in their lives, so the task almost always represents a new, unfamiliar experience.

Proverbs 13:22 says that "a good man leaves an inheritance for his children's children." Instead of balking at the seemingly strange or difficult task of making a will, break the job down into manageable steps. Drafting a will can be divided into two main components: your job and that of your professional financial planner or attorney.

Your job is to answer the questions I'll ask in this chapter. Your advisor's job is to use your responses as a framework for creating a strategic and legally sound document. Together, you can review the will and make changes as the years go by (and in fact, your will *should* be a dynamic, changeable document). Right now, though, your most important—and urgent—step is simply to get into the game.

DECISIONS IN THE ESTATE PLANNING PROCESS

FIGURE 11.1 DIAGRAMS THE ESTATE PLANNING decision process. We have already covered the "Life Overview" component in chapter 10, linking wisdom and wealth under the inheritance umbrella. From there, planning your estate boils down to nothing more than a series of six critical decisions.

1. How Much Do We Leave Our Children?

This question, which we discussed in detail in the last chapter, does more to shape the character and content of your will than anything else. In short, for a couple in their twenties or thirties who have pre-college age children, I recommend that most couples (except for the very wealthy) leave the majority of their assets to their children. It would be unfair to saddle your children's guardians with the financial burden of raising and educating the kids without the benefit of your financial support.

Consider leaving assets to your children via a trust, which their guardians may use until they finish college or reach a certain age. At that point, the assets in the trust could be distributed between the children and charities. Leaving your children financially "set" for life can be dangerous—it can ruin their work ethic, hinder their marriage relationships, and cause self-esteem problems as they are left wondering whether or not they could ever make it on their own.

As your children grow up, reaching certain milestones such as purchasing a home or settling into a career, your perspective on how much to leave them will probably change. Moreover, each child will have different interests, abilities, and financial needs—all of which factor into the estate planning equation.

Leaving your children financially "set" for life can be dangerous.

Finally, if you have children in their forties and fifties who no longer need your assets to supplement their own financial success, you may decide to give most or all of your wealth to charity. On the other hand, if your heirs have demonstrated an ability to make sound business decisions and have a heart for charity, you may want to leave the majority of your assets to them. Under this scenario, it's possible that your children could eventually increase the amount eventually given to charity several times over.

Deciding how much to leave your children is one of the toughest decisions you will ever make. One way to begin determining the right answer, especially if you have adult children, is to begin giving them substantial sums of money each year. Observe how it affects their lifestyle, their marriages, and their giving. Be patient—and watch God work in their lives.

2. How Do I Leave My Assets to My Children?

In the last chapter, we dealt with questions of "form" (as in liquid and non-liquid assets) and "timing" (as in when to give: during your lifetime, or through your will). When you use your will to distribute assets to your children, additional form and timing issues should be considered.

In structuring your children's inheritance, you can either give them the money outright or leave it to them in a trust.

Estate Decision-Making Process

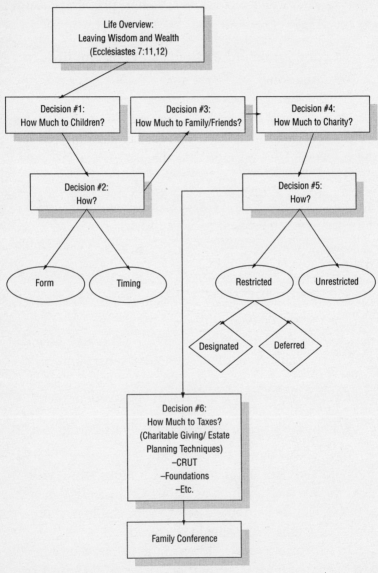

Figure 11.1

Most of our clients decide that, if the parents die while the children are minors, the majority of their assets will be left to the children in a trust. Typically, a trust provides annual income for the health, maintenance, support, and welfare of the trust beneficiaries (that is, the children). If the trustee needs to distribute the corpus (or principal) of the trust for special needs, most trust documents will permit this use of funds.

As your children grow, you may have less of a need to leave your assets in a trust, other than for tax planning purposes. Some people, though, appreciate the security and protection a trust can offer, no matter how old their children are. One of our clients was concerned about his adult children's inexperience and inability to manage money. After deciding how much he wanted to leave to his children, he structured his will so that they would receive one-third of their inheritance upon his death and one-third five years later. The remaining one-third he placed in a trust for his children's lifetime. By this action, our client ensured that his children would have a retirement income as well as an inheritance to pass on to their own children.

If you own a family business, you face a unique set of "form" questions: Is the business value "too much" to pass on to your children? Do your children have the aptitude—or the desire—to take on the responsibility of running a business? Will "handing" your sons (or sons-in-law) the business thwart their God-given drive to provide for their families? Will giving your daughter the family business have a negative impact on her marriage or limit her flexibilty as a mother? Questions like these point to the need for careful consideration in passing on a family business (versus leaving your children assets such as stocks and bonds).

To answer questions like these, start by developing relationships with people who can give you objective advice. Include your pastor's counsel as you make decisions, as he may know your entire family. Next, I suggest reading Leon Danco's books. The founder of The Center for Family Business in Cleveland, Ohio, Danco has written *Inside the Family Business* and *Beyond Survival: A Guide for the Business Owner and His Family*. These books deal with specific principles that can be applied to any business transfer, such as owners not working in the business, the importance of outside directors, the value of having heirs work for outside companies to gain experience before joining the family business, father-son relationships, the need for founders to relinquish total control, and many other valuable insights.

Finally, begin your game plan now. It takes time to prepare a business for sale. It takes even more time to determine whether your children should be part of your family business after your death. A son, for example, may have to serve a ten-year apprenticeship before you can determine whether or not your business is a good fit for him.

3. How Much Do I Want to Leave to Other Family and Friends?

While our children and grandchildren typically receive the majority of our estate assets, generous living may dictate that you broaden your thinking to include other family members or friends, either because they have played an important role in your life or because they have a particular need you would like to meet via your estate. I know of several business owners who have demonstrated their gratitude toward longtime employees by including them in their will. You may also want to make provision for relatives and friends who have served as your spiritual mentors or who provided help and support when you needed it.

Generous living may dictate that you broaden your thinking to include in your will other family members or friends, either because they have played an important role in your life or because they have a particular need you would like to meet.

You can use a number of giving tools and techniques to provide for your family and friends, while also giving to God's kingdom. Joe and Margaret, for example, set up a charitable remainder trust to provide extra income for Margaret's sister, a single mom who has three children to raise and put through college. The trust will give Margaret's sister a monthly income for as long as she lives. Then, upon her death, the remaining balance in the trust will go to charity. If giving to charity is important to you, ask your financial planner or advisor about charitable remainder trusts and other estate planning techniques.

4. How Much Do I Want to Leave to Charity?

There's no doubt about it: When you die, you will have the opportunity to give amounts that would have been impossible during your lifetime. For example, a business owner whose company is worth millions may only draw a modest salary. When he dies, however, if the business is sold, he will have an opportunity to provide adequately for his family with plenty left over to give to his church or other charitable organizations.

Does your will have to contain a charitable bequest? While the Bible does not address this question directly, the scriptural guidelines for giving indicate that, at the minimum, you could tithe through your estate documents. In other words, ten percent (or more) of your assets could go to charity.

When your house is sold as a result of your estate distribution, the profit realized allows an unprecedented opportunity to exercise generous living.

If you think about it, many of your assets have appreciated greatly in value since you originally purchased them. Say you bought your home for $30,000 back in the 1940s, and it's now worth more than $150,000. Because houses are non-liquid assets, most of us cannot tithe "off of the increase" when our homes appreciate. But when your house is sold as a result of your estate distribution, the profit realized allows an unprecedented opportunity to exercise generous living.

5. How Do I Want to Leave My Assets to Charity?

Once you decide how much you want to leave to charity, you need to consider the best way to make the gift. Basically, you can give money to charity in two ways: unrestricted giving and restricted giving.

When you make an unrestricted charitable bequest to a church or organization, you do it with no strings attached. The charity receives the funds outright and can use them however they wish. If you choose to make this type of gift, be sure that the church or organization you give to has consistently demonstrated the ability to exercise wise stewardship of their financial resources.

The other way you can give money outright to a charity is through a restricted gift, which may be *designated* or *deferred*. Designated giving is for a specific purpose. For instance, you may give your church money to establish an inner-city mission or to build an education wing. Deferred giving often takes the form of an endowment. Perhaps you want to establish a scholarship fund for students who want to reach China with the Gospel. You could plan to invest the funds from your estate so that the income and earnings off of the investment can be used to provide scholarships for years (or even generations) to come.

You can also give to charity in trust. Two popular trusts, endorsed by the tax code, are the Charitable Remainder Trust (CRUT) and the Charitable Lead Trust (CLT). In a CRUT, assets are placed in trust and the income beneficiary receives distributions from the trust for a fixed time period. At the end of that time period, the remaining balance goes to charity.

For example, a will could place $500,000 in a CRUT for the benefit of the children. The trust payout could be set at eight percent per year, or $40,000 initially, and then grow if the trust principal increases. At the end of the twenty years, with good investment results, the $500,000 would still be in trust (and possibly would have grown) and must be donated to charity. When assets are placed in a CRUT through an estate, the estate receives a tax deduction—which can stack up to significant estate tax savings.

A Charitable Lead Trust works in a somewhat opposite way. In a CLT, the charity is the income beneficiary and receives the annual income ($40,000 the first year, in the above example), and at the end of the trust period the children receive the trust principal. Depending on factors such as the payout rates to the income beneficiary, the investment earnings of the trust, and the length of time the assets are held in trust, both the CRUT and the CLT provide tax-wise vehicles to accomplish multiple estate planning objectives.

6. How Much Do I Want to Pay in Taxes?

If you and your spouse's combined estates are valued at less than $1.2 million, you should pay *nothing* in estate taxes, according to the provisions in today's tax laws. But if your combined total is more than $1.2 million—and with houses, life insurance, retirement funds, and other assets to consider, you'd be surprised how quickly the numbers can add up—tax planning should be an integral part of your overall estate plan.

Recent tax law changes have made charitable giving one of the primary ways to reduce estate taxes. In addition to giving a lump some of money to charity when you die, your will can establish charitable remainder trusts, charitable lead trusts, and private foundations in order to lower your taxes. You can also take advantage of techniques like irrevocable life insurance trusts or annual gifting programs to reduce the size (and taxability) of your estate.

The legal jargon may sound complicated, but the tax-reducing techniques are actually very simple to implement. Talk with your financial planner or advisor to decide which of these tax-reducing options makes the most sense for you.

Where Do You Go from Here?

Once you've tackled the "big picture" decisions, such as how much to give to your children or charity, you can deal with some of the less philosophical—but no less important—questions. Even if you want to draft the simplest will and leave everything you have to your children, you need to address the following issues:

Who Should Be My Executor?

Your executor is the person responsible for settling your estate. Most people appoint their surviving spouse. As an alternate, a trusted family member or a professional advisor (such as your CPA), could be chosen. Banks, too, have historically performed this function. While leaving the job to a financial institution may mean that you forfeit the personal attention and care a friend or relative would give, you may decide that a bank's impersonal, unbiased approach can work to your family's advantage—at least insofar as relationships are concerned.

Who Should Be the Guardians of Our Children?

More than anything else, choosing a guardian for your minor children can be the most emotional and critical question you will face. Our firm typically counsels people to choose guardians who will raise their children according to the same values and standards that they have—even if that means excluding a close relative.

Before you designate a guardian in your will, make sure that he or she understands and accepts that responsibility. It's also important, as I mentioned earlier, to provide guardians with adequate resources so that raising your children does not become a financial burden.

If I Establish a Trust through My Will, Who Should Be the Trustees?

Many couples whose estates approach or exceed the tax-free limit ($1.2 million in 1997, rising annually to $2 million in 2000) use their wills to establish a residual trust or a family trust to protect their estate (and their heirs) from significant tax consequences. The trustee's job is to manage the assets in the trust, once the executor has finished distributing the estate.

(Executors typically have a relatively short-term responsibility, while trustees may have a job that lasts for several years.)

Trustees are responsible for recording investment income, logging deductions and income distributions, and performing other accounting-related functions. If your spouse shares your values and convictions and is competent to make financial decisions or consult with advisors, he or she is usually the best choice as a trustee. A second choice may be a like-minded sibling who would accept the responsibility of managing the trust on behalf of your surviving spouse and your children.

Will You Have a Testimony?

In his book, *A Life Well Spent*, Russ Crosson recommends including a personal testimony in your will. I agree. As Russ says, your testimony is an explanation of your faith and philosophy, which will be your final statement—your "parting words," if you will—to your posterity when your will is read after your death. There is no better place to take a clear stand about your faith and your commitment to a godly posterity.

Consider including a testimony along these lines to introduce your will:

> I, _____ (your name) of _____ (city, state, country), being of sound mind and with full confidence and trust in my Lord and Savior, Jesus Christ, and his death on the cross and shed blood as an atonement for my sins, and knowing that by faith in his sacrifice on the cross for me I have eternal life, and being desirous of directing what disposition shall be made of the material wealth and earthly possessions with which God in his infinite knowledge, wisdom, and mercy has seen fit to bless and bestow upon me, do therefore make, publish, and declare this to be my last Will and Testament.

Choosing a Financial Planner or Advisor

When it comes to purchasing things such as cars and appliances, many people shop around or do a little detective work before they buy. Choosing a financial planner or advisor requires a similar research effort, but many folks don't know how or where to begin looking. If you keep a few pointers in mind, though, the decision is not as complicated as it might seem.

Begin by interviewing several prospective advisors. First, ask questions about their technical expertise. What degrees do they hold? How much experience do they have? What is their investment or estate planning track record? And, most importantly, does their expertise pertain to your particular needs? Does their client list include people like you?

Next, assess the advisors' wisdom and judgment. You want your advisor to be someone you can trust to make sound choices. As you talk with potential advisors, ask questions about their values, their goals, and their estate planning philosophy. Be sure that they understand your needs and values, and that they can help you answer the "how much" questions from a biblically sound perspective.

Choose a financial advisor whose advice is designed to meet your needs rather than someone who just wants to sell you something.

Finally, find out how they are compensated. Financial planners are paid in three basic ways: fee-only, commission-only, or fee-plus-commissions. I believe that your best option is a fee-only advisor who can give you objective counsel without any conflicts of interest. In other words, choose a financial advisor whose advice is designed to meet your needs (rather than someone who just wants to sell you something). Be sure you clearly understand all the charges involved, and that you are comfortable with them.

Your comfort level is a legitimate issue. When married couples talk with potential advisors, both husband and wife should feel comfortable with and confident in the advisor, especially since he or she is apt to be dealing with only one of you in the future. Likewise, two-way communication is critical: Do you feel that the advisor listened to you? Did you understand what he or she was saying? Do you share the same values and philosophy? Don't make the mistake of thinking that financial planning is strictly practical and emotionless; instead, remember that the "chemistry" between you and your advisor is just as important as his or her financial expertise. Financial needs tend to go hand in hand with mental, emotional, and spiritual issues; be sure that your financial advisor is equipped to offer technical expertise within a broader framework of counseling.

Both husband and wife should feel comfortable with and confident in the advisor, especially since he or she is apt to be dealing with only one of you in the future.

In our firm, financial planners are skilled in assessing our clients' individual situations and walking them through the decisions in the estate planning process. A good financial planner should be able to "quarterback" your financial team, working with CPAs, insurance agents, attorneys, and other advisors to draft an estate plan that effectively meets your needs and goals. Even with smaller estates, where you may have a relationship with only one or two financial professionals, it's a good idea to use the estate planning decision diagram so your advisor(s) understand your decisions and desires.

Having made your decisions and outlined them in your will, you can approach the sixth and final phase in effective estate planning: the family conference. By communicating your desires to your heirs via a family conference, you can encourage your heirs to follow your commitment to generous living and wise stewardship. In the next chapter, you'll learn how to schedule and facilitate a worthwhile family meeting.

Every family gets together to talk about money at some point—usually in the emotion-charged days following a funeral. But by scheduling a family conference early on, you can discuss your estate plan with your heirs and avoid future problems or misunderstandings. Plus, as you share your philosophy, beliefs, and values regarding finances, you can use a family conference to teach, train, and equip your children to handle money wisely.

twelve

A Formal Talk
Holding a Family Conference

W HAT WOULD HAPPEN IF YOU GOT ALL YOUR children and their spouses together in one room and started talking about money? I don't mean money in the abstract; I mean money as in *your* money—and more specifically, what will happen to your money when you die.

Could you do it? Could you, as a parent, handle the practical and emotional challenges of communicating your estate plan to your children? What about them? Would they sit there, in an embarrassed or awkward silence, unwilling to discuss issues related to your mortality? Or would they start clamoring for center stage, grabbing for the bank accounts and the family silver like a pack of wild hyenas?

Having read the first eleven chapters in this book, chances are you have spent considerable time and mental effort thinking about your estate plan as well as your current charitable giving strategies. You have made countless choices and decisions, many of them difficult. You have reached the point where, like most people, you have made your estate documents (wills, trusts, etc.), put them in a safety deposit box, and forgotten about them.

Let me challenge you to take another path. Instead of looking at your estate plan as a document (or set of documents) that can be taken out and dusted off after the Ladies' Altar Guild gives away the flowers from your funeral service, take the time to explain and review your wills in the presence of your heirs. Schedule a family conference.

A family conference is a meeting where you review and discuss your estate plan with your heirs. In addition to going over your wills, you can explain your current and future charitable giving plans, outline your vision for transferring or selling your business, and cover any other areas that might generate future questions or concerns. As a parent, you approach a family conference in one of two ways: You and your spouse can come to the meeting having already made all the decisions and use the gathering as a platform for communicating your distribution plan, or you can voice your thoughts and then entertain discussion from other family members. Both types of meetings can be a positive experience, but if your plan is to leave a large amount to charity and a relatively small amount to your children, you may want to choose the latter option, explaining your rationale and then opening the floor to input from other family members. Using this approach, and by scheduling several successive family conferences, you may be able to educate your children as to the potential pitfalls of a large inheritance and thus equip them to accept what you are doing without bitterness or resentment.

"If you want to really know someone, try sharing an inheritance with them."

Every family has a conference at some point. Usually, this meeting takes place in the emotion-charged days following a funeral, when an attorney, advisor, or some family member summons everyone for the reading of the will. If this is the first exposure your heirs have to the provisions in your estate plan, the revelations could generate tension, bitterness, uncertainty, and misunderstanding. I think Ben Franklin may have said it best when he observed, "If you want to really know someone, try sharing an inheritance with them."

My purpose in writing this chapter is to explain the advantages of a family conference as well as the practical "how-tos" of pulling off a successful meeting. You've reached the final step in effective estate planning; now it's time to put your plan into action.

WHY YOU SHOULD HAVE A FAMILY CONFERENCE

A FAMILY CONFERENCE OFFERS AT LEAST two distinct benefits. First, it facilitates intergenerational communication that allows parents to share their philosophy, beliefs, and values regarding finances, as well as to explain how their financial decisions—both current and deferred—will affect their children. In addition, a family conference can afford an excellent opportunity for financial teaching and training.

Communication

Tom and Jenny began tithing to their church shortly after they were married. As time passed and Tom's income grew, the couple moved into a larger home, bought two new cars, and started saving money to educate their two children. They also continued to give generously, increasing their tithe with each passing year.

Tom and Jenny felt good about the amount they were giving. God had blessed them, financially and in other ways, and they saw their giving as an opportunity to thank him and acknowledge his ownership of their resources. And, as an elder

in their church, Tom liked nothing more than the satisfaction
he and Jenny got as they saw their gifts being used effectively.
Their generosity had helped the church establish an inner-city
outreach, fund summer camp scholarships so teenagers could
hear the Gospel, and break ground on a much-needed Sunday
school wing.

But what Tom and Jenny did not recognize was how their
son, Jack, perceived the situation. As a teenager in a relatively
affluent neighborhood, Jack saw his friends getting stereos,
sports equipment, and even cars when they turned sixteen.
Jack knew his folks would never let him starve, but he wondered why on earth they would give so much money to their
church when there were so many other things they needed.
They didn't even have a decent television!

In time, Jack's curiosity turned into bitterness. He questioned his parents' wisdom and priorities. Eventually, he began
to resent God. And all the while Tom and Jenny went on giving, oblivious to their son's anger and the growing wedge that
was dividing their family.

If they had held a family conference, Tom and Jenny could
have communicated their current giving priorities to their
children, explaining why they wanted to be generous and how
they expected to simultaneously provide for their family's
needs. Under that scenario, Jack would have had a forum to
express his concerns, asking the questions before they became
so consuming. Such intergenerational dialogue could have
prevented—or at least diffused—the divisive situation that
threatened their family harmony.

The family conference is not just an opportunity for parents
to explain their current giving strategies (that is, how much
they currently give to their children and to charity, and why).
The meeting also affords an excellent vehicle whereby parents

can clarify the provisions in their wills. While no one requires parents to communicate their intentions to their children, it's not hard to imagine the difficulty your heirs might have trying to understand your decisions, were you not around to explain them. By neglecting to schedule an "all present" discussion, you can open the door to misunderstandings, questions of motive, bitterness, and disunity among family members when it comes time for the "reading of the will."

While no one requires parents to communicate their intentions to their children, it's not hard to imagine the difficulty your heirs might have trying to understand your decisions, were you not around to explain them.

The communication that marks an effective family conference is a two-way street. As you detail your estate planning decisions, your children will probably have questions and comments. Remember that *money is a tool*. It should never serve as a stumbling block or barrier to your children's faith, nor should it be allowed to drive a wedge between family members. If problems like these surface during your family conference, you may need to re-think some of your decisions and, if necessary, make changes in your wills.

I recall a family conference that took place several years ago. As the parents revealed their distribution plan, the children brought up some significant suggestions as to how and when the estate would be divided. A certain piece of furniture, for example, meant more to the oldest daughter than anyone else, and the family conference gave her a forum for expressing her desire to inherit the piece. Another daughter asked for clarification about a family trust that would be established through the estate.

Money should never be a barrier to family harmony, to effective communication, or to a child coming to Christ.

Without the opportunity for discussion provided by the family conference, the parents' original plan would have caused frustration, uncertainty, and anxiety among the children. But by listening to their heirs, they were able to better explain their estate plan and make adjustments that, ultimately, enhanced the entire family's sense of harmony and joy.

In another situation, the parents had decided to leave assets outright to two of their children and in trust to their third child, who had not demonstrated any ability to handle money wisely and was involved in a reckless, irresponsible lifestyle. When this distribution plan was explained to the children at the family conference, the news came as a tremendous blow to the irresponsible child. The parents realized that significantly greater problems would probably occur under their proposed plan than would be apt to happen if they simply gave each of their children an inheritance outright. Weighing the risks associated with both options, the parents decided to revise their plan.

Again, money is a tool. It should never be a barrier to family harmony, to effective communication, or to a child coming to Christ.

Training

The other major advantage of having a family conference is the vehicle that the gathering represents for financial training. As parents, our job is to teach and train our children to handle money wisely. Our firm has worked with countless clients to schedule and conduct family conferences, and we have been asked to speak on everything from husband-wife relationships to the biblical principles of budgeting.

If your children are in their teens when you schedule your first family conference, you may want to focus on issues like budgeting and understanding the cash flow process. If your kids are older, say in their thirties or forties, you may want to review with them what the Bible says about investing, giving, accumulating money, and training their own children to handle their finances—and all the more so as the distribution of your assets becomes more imminent.

If your family has a history of poor communication or strained relationships, you may have to do some prep work before the conference begins, or plan to hold several successive conferences. Decide what you want to communicate and how you will respond to any foreseeable negative responses. Pray for wisdom and love as you approach your family with this sometimes difficult and uncomfortable subject.

How to Host a Successful Family Conference

PULLING OFF A SUCCESSFUL FAMILY CONFERENCE is not always easy; you need to give careful consideration to whom you invite, when you hold the meeting, and what you intend to accomplish.

Who Should Come?

As you plan your family conference, the first thing you need to decide is *who* you want to come. In addition to you and your spouse, you ought to include your children, their spouses, and, if they are old enough (usually in their teenage years) to understand the issues associated with an inheritance, your grandchildren.

In addition to your children, their spouses, and potentially your grandchildren, you should also invite a third party: a non-family member who can facilitate the discussion without becoming emotionally involved. If you have a strong relationship with a financial planner, CPA, or attorney who shares your estate planning philosophy, he or she might be a logical choice. It's a good idea to select someone your family will regard as a knowledgeable expert. Pick an advisor who has the willingness and ability to raise difficult or sensitive issues and facilitate resolution.

In addition to serving as an objective moderator, your advisor should be qualified to help in the training aspect of your conference. Talk beforehand about the issues you want to cover. The financial advisors in our firm are often called upon by their clients to conduct family conferences. One financial advisor may develop a professional relationship with two or three generations, as different family members raise questions about the overall estate plan and how they should handle or invest their individual inheritances or prepare to do so.

When Should You Get Together?

Next, you need to decide *when* to schedule the conference. In general, I recommend that your first family conference be held whenever a change would warrant it. Families change. Children grow up, get married, change jobs, and have children of their own. Likewise, circumstances change. A charity you support today may become less strategic if it loses sight of its goals or ceases to pursue them effectively. A tax law that triggered some aspect of your estate plan may get overturned or revised, meaning you need to re-think your strategy. Under such a scenario, you may want to revise your estate plan by giving a larger amount to charity or establishing a trust. Changes in your family, your financial circumstances, and estate tax laws all point to the need for frequent and regular intergenerational dialogue.

Estate planning is an ongoing process. Once you have your first family conference, use it as a springboard for future conferences. How often you schedule them will depend on your individual goals and the timeliness of items you need to discuss with your family, as well as the ease with which all of you can get together.

Changes in your family, your financial circumstances, and estate tax laws all point to the need for frequent and regular intergenerational dialogue.

Hypothetically speaking, a family could schedule an initial conference simply to cover some of the basic principles of financial management and estate planning. Using handouts, Scripture references, or the real-life experiences the parents have had, the conference facilitator could help explain the parents' values, beliefs, and financial philosophy.

At the second conference, the facilitator might transition to a more technical discussion. Issues such as the size of the parents' estate, the amounts each child will receive, and how charitable giving will be incorporated into the will could be addressed. Special considerations—such as the establishment and use of a trust—would also be appropriate to cover in this session.

Finally, a third meeting could be held to explain how input from the second conference was incorporated into the will.

Other changes—such as new tax laws or a shift in the size of a parents' estate—could be covered in successive meetings, as the need arises.

What Do You Want to Accomplish?

The final issue you need to address is *what* you want to accomplish through your family conference. One of your primary goals should be to review your estate plan with your heirs so as to clearly communicate your intentions. While many children have a general idea as to their parents' financial picture, very few have a concrete idea as to how the estate will be divided or how much, specifically, they can expect to inherit.

You may also want to explain how your family business will be transferred or sold, or why you decided to distribute your estate to your children in unequal portions. Whatever the specific topics you cover, remember that one of the main benefits of holding a family conference is to foster communication and reduce the potential for future conflict.

Scott and Stephanie had been generous toward their children as they grew, giving them cash at Christmas and helping out with various financial needs from time to time, especially after their grandchildren were born. But Scott and Stephanie rarely spent money on themselves. As far as their children knew, their resources were "adequate"—but certainly not plentiful.

When Scott and Stephanie's financial advisor outlined the provisions in their will at a recent family conference, the children were stunned. Their parents' estate was larger than they had ever imagined. Suddenly, future management of these resources became a pressing concern. The children had to prepare themselves to handle the inheritance wisely.

With the coming $8- to $14-trillion inheritance bonanza I told you about in chapter 3, stories like this one are becoming increasingly common. And the money isn't coming from America's wealthiest families; instead, the inheritance numbers are piling up as a result of long-term savings accounts, life insurance policies, retirement funds, appreciated real estate, and other assets commonly held by the "middle class." Like Scott and Stephanie, you may not think of yourself as "rich," but your estate will probably be big enough to warrant your children's attention.

As you communicate your plan to your heirs, you might want to use a transgenerational flow chart similar to the one in figure 12.1. Your chart can include as little or as much detail as you want; in general, it should describe the generational flow of your assets and, potentially, the dollar amounts involved. (Typically, such concrete financial information can be shared as your children reach their twenties and begin to make their own way in the world.)

Using a chart like this one, you can attach specific dollar amounts to each of your heirs and explain how the inheritance will be distributed. If assets are being left in a trust, for example, you will need to explain how the trust will work. Your children (and grandchildren, if applicable) need to know what they can expect, and when they will receive it, in order to establish and maintain their own strategic financial plans.

In addition to reviewing your estate plan, your goals for the family conference might include current gifting strategies, both to your heirs and to charity. If you plan to take advantage of the annual gift exclusion I talked about in chapter 10, let your children know how much you plan to give them every year. As your kids work to figure out how they will pay for education, vacations, housing, and other family needs, factoring in an annual gift could make a significant difference in their plans. Also, if you plan to maintain or increase your current or deferred charitable giving, letting your children know about it can help ward off a situation like the one Tom and Jenny faced with their son.

Your children might also benefit from reviewing your charitable giving strategies if you include them in the decision. Some of our clients have made giving a family affair,

Transgenerational Planning

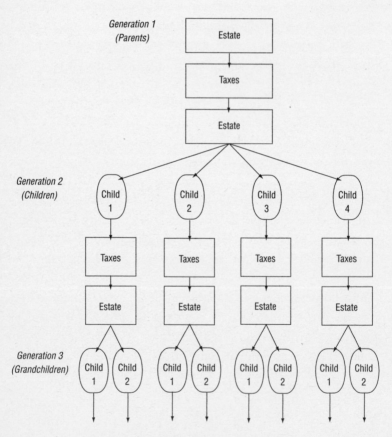

Figure 12.1

choosing the charities and ministry organizations they want to give to on a collective basis. If your kids are involved in the decision-making process, they will gain firsthand exposure to the generosity process, and they will be more apt to continue the giving traditions you have established.

SEIZING THE OPPORTUNITY

WHILE THIS BOOK HAS FOCUSED ON giving, you cannot give unless you are watching for opportunities to do so. Whether you have crafted an estate plan, an investment strategy, or something as seemingly routine as a family budget, all your efforts will count for nothing if you miss out on the opportunities that come with generous living.

In the final pages of this book, I want to challenge you to pay attention to the opportunities God gives us today. Look at what he is doing. Watch the world around you. And then see how you can get in on the action, reaping the relationships, the rewards, and even the miracles our heavenly Father has to offer.

Never before in the history of time have the challenges and opportunities for using wealth strategically been so great. But giving doesn't just change the world. Generosity changes us, filling our lives with rewards like peace, security, and true financial freedom.

thirteen

Opportunity Knocks

Solving the Wealth Paradox

"OF ALL THE PEOPLE WHO HAVE EVER LIVED, HALF of them are alive today."

"Are you kidding?" I looked at Bill Bright, amazed by the statistic he had just shared. I found it almost mind-boggling: Six billion of us populate the earth today—fully half of the twelve billion people born since the beginning of time. Stacked against the push by Campus Crusade and other ministries to complete the Great Commission by the year 2000, the population figures take on a whole new significance. Many need to be reached with the Gospel—can we really hope to get the job done?

On the one hand, fulfilling the Great Commission seems almost impossible, based on the sheer magnitude of the task. On the other hand, we really do have what it takes. The financial resources are there, for starters. As we saw in chapter 3, Americans are richer than ever before, making money even faster than we can spend it. With a minimum of sacrifice or risk, we could come up with an extra $100 billion each year for charitable giving. Not only that, but 80 percent of the world's evangelical wealth is in North America—and the total represents way more than enough to fund the fulfillment of the Great Commission.

Equally significant is the "global village" aspect of our modern culture. The much-hyped technological revolution that brought computers and the Internet into our living rooms has run parallel to a monumental shift in the world's political landscape. Today, with the exception of some parts of the Muslim world, there are no real political barriers. Aided by the media, we can have instant access to virtually every part of the globe.

Spiritually, too, the possibilities are limitless. We are living in a climate of spiritual openness and receptivity that—at least for our generation—is beyond compare. I've already told you about the explosive growth taking place in the Promise Keepers movement, as well as the highly leveraged and effective nature of evangelism projects such as the *Jesus* film. Similar reports of mass spiritual revivals are garnering attention across the country, particularly in our colleges and seminaries. As Dr. John Woodbridge, a church historian and professor at Trinity Evangelical Divinity School, puts it, "In 25 years of teaching I've never seen anything like this . . . It is a wonderful work of the Spirit of God."[1]

It's a move and a message that is taking root around the world, even in traditionally Muslim and Communist strongholds. In Iraq, for instance, the *Jesus* film has been shown three times on national television since the Persian Gulf War. And in China, where there were only one million known Christians in 1950, some 28,000 people convert to Christianity each day, and, according to official communist projections, there will be 100 million believers in Communist China by the year 2000.

Statistics and projections like these make for an incredible window of opportunity for evangelism. Coupled with the financial, technological, and political breakthroughs the world has seen in recent years, we have to stop and ask ourselves, Are we taking advantage of this opportunity? God is obviously at work. Are we getting in on his action?

THE WEALTH PARADOX

IF WE FIND OURSELVES MISSING GOD'S opportunities or standing as spectators to the action he directs, it may be because we are caught up in what I call the "Wealth Paradox." This paradox is based on two faulty assumptions and two corresponding realities:

1. *Assumption:* When you accumulate money, you will enjoy greater freedom and satisfaction. Because of that, a better relationship with God and greater opportunities to serve him will follow.

Reality: Accumulation of wealth complicates life. A close relationship with God may become more difficult to maintain.

2. *Assumption:* When you accumulate money, you will have freedom from fear.

Reality: Accumulation of wealth brings a new fear: the fear of losing what you have.

Missing the Relationship

The first issue, or risk, associated with the wealth paradox is that you will miss hearing God's voice and therefore miss out on a deeper relationship with him than you might otherwise have enjoyed. The risk of a missed relationship is a direct result of thinking that more money will buy us more freedom and satisfaction, when the reality is that money tends to make things more complicated.

Here's what I mean. When Judy and I were first married we lived in an eight- by thirty-foot trailer. You could wash the dishes, sit on the pot, and make the bed almost without moving.

Judy recently reminded me that when she set up the ironing board, it took up the entire living room and all of the kitchen as well. We had very little money—and because of that, we had very few choices. Where to eat out was not a decision we had to make; we simply could not afford to eat out at all. Likewise, vacations, new cars, clothing, and all the other things that might have clamored for our attention were hardly considerations, since we could not have purchased them had we even wanted to.

Over the years, as our income grew, we began to face all sorts of decisions. Houses, vacations, schooling, and a variety of other spending options crowded the picture. Once we could afford to take vacations, buy a bigger home, or get a new car, we moved from asking ourselves "*Can* we afford it?" to "*Should* we buy it?" Instead of having more freedom, we actually felt like we had less!

It doesn't matter whether you make $20,000 or $200,000 per year. You will always have choices to make. More money simply means more choices.

Since there are always unlimited ways to spend limited dollars, it doesn't matter whether you make $20,000 or $200,000 per year. You will always have choices to make. More money simply means more choices. And more choices mean more complexity, more confusion, and more time spent mulling over our options. Taken together, all these things add up to less freedom.

Remember the church in Laodicea? As I mentioned in chapter 5, the Laodiceans fell into the prosperity trap, allowing their wealth to replace spiritual sensitivity. In Revelation 3:20 we get a clue as to what happened: "Here I am!" Jesus says. "I stand at the door and knock. If anyone hears my voice and opens the door, I will come in and eat with him, and he with me."

The Lord was not about to push his way into the Laodiceans' lives. Likewise, he will not intrude in our affairs. Instead, he stands at the door and knocks. When the busyness of our lives—our jobs, our houses, our schooling and vacation choices—captivates our attention, we will not be able to hear God's voice. He will stand at the door and knock, but we will not hear him above the noise. We will miss his voice—and, ultimately, the relationship he offers.

Falling Victim to Fear

The second major risk associated with the wealth paradox is that you will fall victim to fear. In this case, the paradox is that when you accumulate money, you imagine that it will bring you freedom from fear. In reality, though, you reap a new kind of fear: the fear of losing what you have. As a result, you may wind up missing God's opportunities.

If God is always with us, then he can preserve and protect us. He can also preserve and protect our wealth.

In chapter 7, I told you what happened to the twelve spies the Israelites sent to scout out the Promised Land. All twelve agreed that it was a lush and lovely place, but only two were willing to take possession of it. The rest were paralyzed by fear.

They saw the giants who inhabited Canaan—and that was enough to make them turn tail and run. They did not want to lose their lives.

The Israelites' mistake was the same one we often make today: They left God out of the equation. Dr. Bruce Wilkinson, the president of Walk Thru the Bible Ministries, says when we experience fear it's because of one thing: We do not believe in the presence of God. We do not believe he is always with us. But Scripture promises otherwise: "The Lord your God will be with you wherever you go" (Joshua 1:9).

If God is always with us, then he can preserve and protect us. He can also preserve and protect our wealth. Jesus understood this truth and tried to communicate it to his disciples in his well-known Sermon on the Mount. The following passage is excerpted from Matthew 6 as retold in Eugene Peterson's *The Message*:

> Don't hoard treasure down here where it gets eaten by moths and corroded by rust or—worse!—stolen by burglars. Stockpile treasure in heaven, where it's safe from moth and rust and burglars. It's obvious, isn't it? The place where your treasure is, is the place you will most want to be, and end up being. . . .
>
> Your eyes are windows into your body. If you open your eyes wide in wonder and belief, your body fills up with light. If you live squinty-eyed in greed and distrust, your body is a dank cellar. If you pull the blinds on your windows, what a dark life you will have!
>
> You can't worship two gods at once. Loving one god, you'll end up hating the other. Adoration of one breeds contempt for the other. You can't worship God and money both.

If you decide for God, living a life of God-worship, it follows that you don't fuss about what's on the table at mealtimes or whether the clothes in your closet are in fashion. There is far more to your life than the food you put in your stomach, more to your outer appearance than the clothes you hang on your body. Look at the birds, free and unfettered, not tied down to a job description, careless in the care of God. And you count far more to him than birds . . .

What I'm trying to do here is to get you to relax, to not be so preoccupied with *getting*, so you can respond to God's *giving*. . . .Give your entire attention to what God is doing right now, and don't get worked up about what may or may not happen tomorrow. God will help you deal with whatever hard things come up when the time comes.

In this passage, Jesus offers the right perspective on wealth—and, by extension, the right perspective on how to enjoy a relationship with God and deal with your fears. When you recognize that God owns it all, you will no longer fear losing anything, because you do not own anything!

When you recognize that God owns it all, you will no longer fear losing anything, because you do not own anything!

Peterson's language communicates biblical truths in a powerful way. Four things, in particular, strike me about this passage. First, Jesus says its *obvious* that we will want to be where our treasure is. Next, he likens greedy living to living in a *dank cellar*. Third, he emphasizes the life of freedom that we will enjoy when we adopt the right perspective: we will be *careless in the care of God*. And finally, the issue is not so much our giving as it is our ability to *relax and respond to God's giving*. The picture painted by concepts and words such as these is vividly clear: God does not ask us to give because he needs the money. Rather, he wants us to give because generosity—using material wealth for eternal purposes—is the key ingredient in experiencing a life of freedom and joy.

A friend of mine once wondered why people were so reluctant to face death. After hearing me speak one day on the importance of giving to God's kingdom, the proverbial lightbulb went on in her head. Suddenly she understood the situation: "People do not want to die because they do not have any treasure in heaven," she said. "They have not sent it on ahead!"

As long as we allow the fear of losing money to restrict our generosity, we will never be able to respond to the opportunities God gives us. We will always hoard our treasure here on earth, instead of stockpiling it in heaven. Not only will this attitude limit our relationship with God, it will keep us forever captive to fear. The only way to change things is to give.

WHAT YOU GET WHEN YOU GIVE

ENCOURAGING YOU TO GIVE HAS BEEN my primary emphasis in this book. Why? In part, it's because I want you to experience freedom from fear, to develop a heart for God, and to grasp an eternal perspective. But giving offers much more than these things. When you exercise and experience generous living, you stand to reap God's incredible blessings.

I remember watching Richard Nixon's funeral on television some years ago. Billy Graham got up to speak, and, with the whole world watching—including the four former presidents and scores of ambassadors and diplomats in attendance at the ceremony—I wondered what the evangelist would say. From a political standpoint, some might have considered it totally inappropriate to share a bold and unapologetic gospel message.

But that is exactly what Billy Graham did. In a tone and with a gentleness that matched the dignity of the occasion, Graham outlined God's plan for our salvation—before a worldwide television audience! People who might never have tuned in to witness a Graham crusade were watching on that day. God gave Billy Graham the opportunity of a lifetime.

Why did Graham respond to that opportunity? His relationship with God—a relationship that left no room for fear—allowed the evangelist to hear the Lord's voice and respond to his gentle knock of opportunity. In the same manner, our giving can open the door to a deeper and stronger relationship with the Lord. It allows us to break free of the prosperity trap—and all the noise, confusion, and fear it holds—so we can hear God and recognize what he wants us to do.

God wants us to give because generosity—using material wealth for eternal purposes—is the key ingredient in experiencing a life of freedom and joy.

In a passage from the Sermon on the Mount in Matthew 6, Jesus tells us to give our "entire attention to God and to what God is doing right now, and don't get worked up about what may or may not happen tomorrow." When we give God our attention—as Billy Graham did—we will reap his rewards. Likewise, when we give our time, our prayers, our good works, and our money, our generosity will make a difference—both on earth and in heaven.

There is no doubt in my mind that how we live on earth will impact our lives in eternity. While salvation is a free gift (and there is nothing we can do to earn it), the Bible makes it clear that our works—our prayers, our actions, our gifts—will one day be taken into account. (See, for example, 2 Cor. 5:9–10; Gal. 6:7–9; 1 Cor. 3:9–15; Rev. 22:12.) Like the wise servants we talked about in chapter 8—the ones who strategically managed their master's money—all of us long to hear God say, "Well done, good and faithful servant." How, then, does this mean we should live?

Dr. Bruce Wilkinson addresses the subject of eternal rewards more effectively than anyone I have heard in recent years. One of the passages he points us toward is 1 Timothy 6:17–19:

> Command those who are rich in this present world not to be arrogant nor to put their hope in wealth, which is so uncertain, but to put their hope in God, who richly provides us with everything for our enjoyment. Command them to do good, to be rich in good deeds, and to be generous and willing to share. In this way they will lay up treasure for themselves as a firm foundation for the coming age, so that they may take hold of the life that is truly life.

There can be no question as to how God wants us to live. He commands us to be generous. But that's not all. He promises that we will reap according to what we sow—and many times over, at that. As Matthew 13:23 puts it, the Lord will cause the fruit we sow to grow thirty-, sixty-, and one hundredfold.

To give you a better picture of the kind of return we are talking about, I like to think about it in investment terms. In my business we deal with investments all the time, and a return of twelve percent, over time, is considered phenomenal. A thirtyfold return means getting something thirty times over—which translates into a 3,000 percent return on an annual basis! Imagine (if you can) making an investment that promises to grow at 3,000, 6,000, and 10,000 percent for all eternity! Now that is *truly* phenomenal!

Rewards like these are beyond calculation or comprehension. Yet they are real. The small blessings we see on earth are a mere foretaste of the bounty to come. Remember Ruby's story? She went from inheriting a business that had not paid its bills for three years to being able to give away $20,000 every month—all because she listened to God when he told her to give!

Stories like Ruby's are miracles. But for those who take advantage of God's eternal interest rates, they will be commonplace. God is ready and anxious to reward us: "Behold," Jesus says in Revelation 22:12, "I am coming soon! My reward is with me, and I will give to everyone according to what he has done."

Have you ever wondered what it will be like to stand before the Lord as he evaluates what you have done? Go back and read Matthew 6:19–34. Think about what really counts.

Historically speaking, we are at a crossroads. Never before have the challenges—and the opportunities—for using wealth strategically been so great. My purpose in writing this book has been to give you the tools and techniques you need to take advantage of these opportunities. Perhaps, like Frank and Shirley, you are working yourself out of a tough financial situation and you want to begin tithing on a regular basis. Or possibly you are like Jack, the young doctor, and you want to cap your lifestyle so that you can get to the "would give" level.

Maybe you have simply accumulated enough wealth that you are thinking about how you should distribute it to your family or to charity.

Regardless of your particular situation, generous living offers financial peace of mind and freedom from fear. Additionally, it gives you the opportunity to be a strategic part of God's work during this critical time in history. And, as you think about your estate and the legacy you want to leave to the next generation, generous living opens the door to wisdom and an understanding of good stewardship.

If you have not done so already, start stockpiling your treasure in heaven. Send it on ahead. You'll be glad you did—and all the more as you begin to watch God's miracles unfold.

notes

Chapter Three

1. Harvey D. Shapiro, "The Coming Inheritance Bonanza," *Institutional Investor,* June 1994, 143.

2. Ibid., 145.

3. Keith Brown with John W. Hoover, *Faith Promise and Beyond* (Kearney, Neb.: Morris, 1995), 1–3.

4. Brown, *Faith Promise and Beyond,* 4–5.

5. John L. Ronsvalle and Sylvia Ronsvalle, *The State of Church Giving through 1994* (Champaign, IL: Empty Tomb, Inc., 1995), 12–14.

6. Claude Rosenberg Jr., *Wealthy and Wise* (Boston, Mass.: Little, Brown, and Company, 1994), 13–17.

7. Christine Dugas, "Paying Off Cards Saves a Bundle," *USA Today,* 27 September 1996, sec. B, p. 7.

Chapter Six

1. Sandra Block, "Even Millionaires Sweat Retirement," *USA Today,* 21 May 1996, sec. B, p. 1.

Chapter Seven

1. Scott Boeck and Marcy E. Mullins, "Money or Happiness?" *USA Today,* 8 July 1996, sec. B., p. 1.

2. Henry T. Blackaby and Claude V. King, *Experiencing God: Knowing and Doing the Will of God* (Nashville: LifeWay Press, 1990), 109.

Chapter Thirteen

1. Nancy Gibbs, "The Message of Miracles," *Time,* April 10, 1995, 68.

Acknowledgments

It is with deep gratitude that I recognize two major contributors to this book. Jodie Berndt, who made such a contribution that she is listed on the front as a writer and, basically, co-author. It is a joy working with Jodie. She is a remarkable woman who manages a family of four children and a busy husband, and in the midst of it all, writes so professionally.

Additionally, Fran LaMattina has made a significant contribution to anything that I have done publicly since she began working with me several years ago. Without her constant encouragement, I probably would never have written again. Thank you, Fran, for your encouragement and for your unwavering support. It means a lot.

I also want to thank Russ Crosson and Scott Houser, two Ronald Blue and Co. (RBC) Partners who believe in the precepts of stewardship and generous living. They have contributed a great deal to the content of several chapters of this work.

Finally, the most important woman in my life is my wife, who has borne with me through many books as well as through the development of RBC, the business that God has given to me. I can truthfully say that apart from the Lord Jesus, she is the most significant person in my life—past, present, or future. God has blessed me abundantly with a wonderful wife.

Steps to Peace with God

 ### Step 1 God's Purpose:
Peace and Life

God loves you and wants you to experience peace and life—abundant and eternal.

The Bible Says . . .

". . . we have peace with God through our Lord Jesus Christ." Romans 5:1

"For God so loved the world that He gave His only begotten Son, that whoever believes in Him should not perish but have everlasting life." John 3:16

". . . I have come that they may have life, and that they may have it more abundantly." John 10:10b

Since God planned for us to have peace and the abundant life right now, why are most people not having this experience?

 ### Step 2 Our Problem:
Separation

God created us in His own image to have an abundant life. He did not make us as robots to automatically love and obey Him, but gave us a will and a freedom of choice.

We chose to disobey God and go our own willful way. We still make this choice today. This results in separation from God.

Our choice results in separation from God.

The Bible Says . . .

"For all have sinned and fall short of the glory of God." Romans 3:23

"For the wages of sin is death, but the gift of God is eternal life in Christ Jesus our Lord." Romans 6:23

Our Attempts

Through the ages, individuals have tried in many ways to bridge this gap ... without success ...

The Bible Says ...

"There is a way that seems right to man, but in the end it leads to death." Proverbs 14:12

"But your iniquities have separated you from God; and your sins have hidden His face from you, so that He will not hear." Isaiah 59:2

There is only one remedy for this problem of separation.

Step 3 God's Remedy: The Cross

Jesus Christ is the only answer to this problem. He died on the Cross and rose from the grave, paying the penalty for our sin and bridging the gap between God and people.

The Bible Says ...

"... God is on one side and all the people on the other side, and Christ Jesus, Himself man, is between them to bring them together ..." 1 Timothy 2:5

"For Christ also has suffered once for sins, the just for the unjust, that He might bring us to God ..." 1 Peter 3:18a

"But God demonstrates His own love for us in this: While we were still sinners, Christ died for us." Romans 5:8

God has provided the only way ... we must make the choice ...

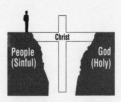

Step 4 Our Response:
Receive Christ

We must trust Jesus Christ and receive Him by personal invitation.

The Bible Says . . .

"Behold, I stand at the door and knock. If anyone hears My voice and opens the door, I will come in to him and dine with him, and he with Me." Revelation 3:20

"But as many as received Him, to them He gave the right to become children of God, even to those who believe in His name." John 1:12

". . . if you confess with your mouth the Lord Jesus and believe in your heart that God has raised Him from the dead, you will be saved." Romans 10:9

Are you here . . . or here?

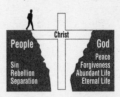

Is there any good reason why you cannot receive Jesus Christ right now?

How to receive Christ:

1. Admit your need (I am a sinner).
2. Be willing to turn from your sins (repent).
3. Believe that Jesus Christ died for you on the Cross and rose from the grave.
4. Through prayer, invite Jesus Christ to come in and control your life through the Holy Spirit. (Receive Him as Lord and Savior.)

What to Pray:

Dear Lord Jesus,

I know that I am a sinner and need Your forgiveness. I believe that You died for my sins. I want to turn from my sins. I now invite You to come into my heart and life. I want to trust and follow You as Lord and Savior.

In Jesus' name. Amen.

_____   _____
Date   Signature

God's Assurance:
His Word

If you prayed this prayer,

The Bible Says...

"For 'whoever calls upon the name of the Lord will be saved.'"
Romans 10:13

Did you sincerely ask Jesus Christ to come into your life? Where is He right now? What has He given you?

"For it is by grace you have been saved, through faith—and this is not from yourselves, it is the gift of God—not by works, so that no one can boast." Ephesians 2:8,9

The
Bible Says...

"He who has the Son has life; he who does not have the Son of God does not have life. These things I have written to you who believe in the name of the Son of God, that you may know that you have eternal life, and that you may continue to believe in the name of the Son of God." 1 John 5:12–13, NKJV

Receiving Christ, we are born into God's family through the supernatural work of the Holy Spirit who indwells every believer…this is called regeneration or the "new birth."

This is just the beginning of a wonderful new life in Christ. To deepen this relationship you should:

1. Read your Bible every day to know Christ better.
2. Talk to God in prayer every day.
3. Tell others about Christ.
4. Worship, fellowship, and serve with other Christians in a church where Christ is preached.
5. As Christ's representative in a needy world, demonstrate your new life by your love and concern for others.

God bless you as you do.

Billy Graham

If you want further help in the decision you have made, write to:
Billy Graham Evangelistic Association P.O. Box 779, Minneapolis, Minnesota 55440-0779